Praise

How I wish I'd read this book when I was just starting out in my career! Using examples from a variety of women leaders, as well as the author's own experiences, *Never Get Their Coffee: Empowering Fearless Leadership* provides a template for developing skills and successfully navigating difficult situations. Tackling subjects as wide-ranging as the trap of getting coffee and ordering lunches to how to lead in times of crisis, author Lakisha Ann Woods offers down-to-earth, actionable advice for women who want to continue growing throughout their work lives. This book will serve as a reference for those who face obstacles or want to take on more responsibility, no matter where they are in their career path.

Denise Dersin
Executive Editor
Pro Builder Magazine

Mrs. Woods' book is a must read for men and women at all levels of their career. Her book masterfully gives practical career advice while also reinforcing the proven benefits of diversity on an organizations profitability while also urging us all to examine how our unconscious bias affects hiring, promotions and policy decisions."

David Mack
Commander, US Navy

Exactly the kind of book the world needs right now! Never Get Their Coffee is the de facto manuscript on the next generation of female leadership and what that can and should look like.

Shawn Johal | Business Growth Coach, Elevation Leaders

Impactful! An excellent book about the future of female leadership!

Tamara Nall | CEO & Founder, The Leading Niche

Lakisha Woods' Never Get Their Coffee is a profound examination of how women are culturally fed the beliefs that hold them back from achieving their own great success stories. Thought-provoking!

Mark Nureddine | CEO of Bull Outdoor Products and the bestselling author of Pocket Mentor

Lakisha Woods is a prime example of the new generation of female leaders that is rising through the ranks and proving female leadership has a huge value to any organization. Articulate, intelligent and wildly talented in her storytelling, this is not an author you're going to want to overlook.

Orad Elkayam | Founder, Mogi Group

This book is a must read for anyone looking to understand the female perspective on leadership and the roadblocks that we, as a society, consciously and unconsciously construct against them.

Judy Dinelle | Building Ambassador, 84 Lumber Co.

All too often, women have limited leadership opportunities despite being highly qualified for these roles. It's time to change that narrative, and it all starts here, with books like Never Get Their Coffee.

Shawn E. Boynes | Executive Director, American Association for Anatomy

Lakisha Woods has accomplished something remarkable here. Her book is both an analysis of the bias and prejudice that women face each and every day (in and outside of the office), but also WHY this prejudice happens in the first place. What's more, she does it in a humble, self-reflective, first-person manner that truly brings it to life through everyday examples. Her manuscript is a hopeful vision of what we can do to change the narrative for future generations of women the world over.

Mark Masson | Partner, Axiom Consulting Partners

Never Get Their Coffee is one of the best books I've read this year! Powerful, concise and chalk full of research...I was blown away!

Rebecca Ramsey | Business Development Executive, Eventeq

https://lakishawoods.com/bonus

https://lakishawoods.com/bonus

NEVER
GET THEIR
COFFEE

EMPOWERING
FEARLESS LEADERSHIP

Lakisha Ann Woods

Leaders
Press

Leaders
Press

ISBN 978-1-63735-115-4 (pbk)
ISBN 978-1-63735-116-1 (ebook)

SIMON &
SCHUSTER

Print Book Distributed by Simon & Schuster
1230 Avenue of the Americas
New York, NY 10020

Library of Congress Control Number: 2021913219

The trademarks, brands, and references to companies
including logos of various companies are used in this text
for nominative purposes when discussing these companies.
These companies do not sponsor or endorse this book, its
author, or its publisher.

Dedication

To my daughter Maya, who inspires me every day to keep moving forward and to be fearless.

Contents

Introduction xi

Chapter 1: It's Bigger Than Coffee 1

Chapter 2: You Deserve It, Please Stop Apologizing 9

Chapter 3: I Am Who You Made Me 19

Chapter 4: The Dirty Secret: Image IS Everything 37

Chapter 5: Communication Skills are Key 49

Chapter 6: Leading in a Time of Crisis 61

Chapter 7: Drinks with the Boys 71

Chapter 8: Unconscious Bias 83

Chapter 9: It's All About the Laws 105

Chapter 10: Did You Make the Ask? 121

Chapter 11: Leading as a Woman of Color 129

Chapter 12: Practice Wellness 141

Epilogue: Life Lessons from My Three-Year-Old 153

Acknowledgements 157

About the Author 159

Introduction— Having It All

Recently, I was having a cup of coffee with a friend and we began to discuss the challenges for women in leadership. She sipped her Skinny Cinnamon Dolce Latté and said, "Why is it a news story when women just want normal success?"

I thought back to the start of my career, working until 9:00 on Friday nights while my friends were already at happy hour. My early jobs allowed me to experience profound professional success but, time and again, I felt as if I was experiencing personal failure. Back then, I sat awake at night, thinking of the countless times I'd been called intimidating, too strong, and too successful.

I think of the future leader who faces her own questions about professional success and how it impacts her personal life. Is there really a direct correlation between success at work and likeability? Personally, I believe a happy life is about balance. Sometimes women have a need to feel liked and, in turn, may make decisions at work that hinder professional growth. An example I often see is when a woman allows a man to take credit for her idea or work product in an effort to please him. The end result is often the man being elevated to higher-level positions while the woman is left wondering why she was passed over. I try to focus on producing quality work, ensuring my team has what they need to be successful, and also making sure the right people receive the credit for our accomplishments.

Consider the incredibly complex criteria for women who want to *have it all*:

- Friends
- A successful career
- A family

In her book *My Beloved World*, Sonia Sotomayor says, "But as for the possibility of 'having it all,' career and family, with no sacrifice to either, that is a myth we would do well to abandon, together with the pernicious notion that a woman who chooses one or the other is somehow deficient."[1] Listening to my friend frame the idea of women wanting normal things as news gave me flashbacks. I recalled countless conversations during which I had been given so-called friendly advice that I would have to choose between finding the right man and having a successful career. All this seemed to put a new perspective on the media's recent coverage of gender equality.

News Stories

The #MeToo movement

The story: Women no longer want to be sexually assaulted or harassed in their personal or professional lives.

    The reality: It's normal to want to feel safe out in public or in your workplace.

Record number of women running for office

The story: In the U.S., a democratic government "of the people, by the people, and for the people," a record number of women have been elected to Congress.

---

[1] Sotomayor, Sonia. 2016. *In My Beloved World*, 233. New York: Alfred A. Knopf.

The reality: In a country in which, according to the U.S. census, approximately 51 percent of the population is female, the 2020 election saw a record number of women elected to national office in the United States.[2] This means 140 of the 535 seats—or 27 percent—in Congress and the Senate combined are held by women. According to Pew Research, that represents a 50 percent increase from the 96 women who were serving in the 112th Congress ten years prior.[3]

This increase in female elected officials got extensively more coverage in the previous election when you would often see headlines that read "The Year of the Woman." If you followed the media coverage at that time, you would have thought women had achieved significant gains in equal representation. But according to 2019 data from the World Economic Forum, "the United States still lags well behind much of the world when it comes to female representation," ranking behind at least seventy other countries on a list compiled by the Inter-Parliamentary Union.[4]

Women all over the world are starting to realize *en masse* that it's okay to want more and, in this case, "more" simply means they are seeking what men have had since the beginning of time: *a seat at the table.* This book is about training the next generation to know better from the start.

---

[2] "U.S. Census Quick Facts Table." United States Census. https://www.census.gov/quickfacts/fact/table/US/LFE046219. Accessed August 22, 2021.

[3] Blazina, Carrie, and Drew DeSilver."A Record Number of Women Are Serving in the 117th Congress." Pew Research Center. *Pew Research Center,* January 22, 2021. http://www.pewresearch.org/fact-tank/2021/01/15/a-record-number-of-women-are-serving-in-the-117th-congress/. Accessed August 22, 2021.

[4] Thornton, Alex. "These Countries Have the Most Women in Parliament." *World Economic Forum*, February 12, 2019. https://www.weforum.org/agenda/2019/02/chart-of-the-day-these-countries-have-the-most-women-in-parliament/. Accessed August 22, 2021.

It's raising our children, grandchildren, nieces, and nephews as equals. For true equality to happen, the training must start at birth—not just for girls and boys, but for moms and dads, aunts and uncles, grandparents, and neighbors. The whole community must set the standard for how we treat our children to ensure that, by the time they enter the workforce, equality has already been ingrained into their identity. We must not only tell our young girls to strive for greatness and work hard. We also need to teach our young men to value women who achieve success and see them as equals.

It's up to all of us to ensure the next generation of women do not feel the need to bypass higher roles because they've been trained to play it safe. I want to see a better world for friends, neighbors, and especially for my three-year-old daughter—and I know I can't do it alone. This book is about taking time to recognize that women are capable of so much more than what society has traditionally expected of them. Let this serve as a challenge to our mothers, daughters, sisters, and girlfriends to wake up at the beginning of the week, look at themselves in the mirror, and say, "I will never get their coffee."

Reflections on My Father

What motivates us to succeed? When I was young, my father's habit of telling me what I could not do often drove me to try to prove him wrong. I always wanted to prove him wrong, so I continued to try harder. My mother served a traditional role as a positive supporter of my aspirations. She always told me I could do or be anything I wanted. Today, I wonder if I would have worked as hard without my father's provocations in my ear.

My father passed away when I was 24, and my life came to a screeching halt. I was a daddy's girl through and through, and to lose my father to a heart attack at such a young age was devastating. As I reflect on all those years when he warned me to be cautious, telling me I was too young to start a business or too young to run a production company, I know in his heart he was trying to protect me. However, his messages of protection are what drove me to try harder to succeed. I was always trying to prove my father wrong, not prove my mother right.

I wonder these days if I would have achieved my career success had I not had both the positive and negative messages in my head telling me how to move forward. We need to hear that we can be a success, but we also need to hear that we should double-check our work. I always ask my mother what she and my father put in the water because both my sister and I were driven to start working as soon as possible. When my sister was 14, she began a job at a local amusement park in Utah. At the time, you could legally work at age 14. My birthday is on Christmas Day, and when I turned 16, we lived in Alaska. I walked into the only business open on Christmas Day—a movie theater—and asked for a job. I worked there throughout high school. My parents were traditional middle class. They gave us everything we needed and most of what we wanted. But both my sister and I could not wait to make our own money; we never wanted to take from our parents what we believed we could earn on our own. We were both very driven then and still are to this day, and we challenge ourselves to do and be more professionally. I am so grateful to have had parents to love and protect us and train us up to be good people and positive examples in the workforce.

I am grateful still to have my mother with me, to love and shape me as I continue to grow as a mother and a professional. And of course, I always wish my father was still with us and had not passed away so young. It would have been amazing if he could have witnessed big moments like my wedding or when we were blessed with my daughter Maya. Also, the small moments, like the family road trips we took crossing the country and sharing the simple experiences in life. I wish I could tell my father I now understand the feedback he offered, and that his words are what drive me to succeed every day.

Never Get Their Coffee is a call to action. It is a challenge for young girls and women to be proud to see themselves as the CEOs of tomorrow, and to stop apologizing for wanting normal things. However, this book isn't just for women—it's for anyone who wants to shape the future behavior and thought patterns of men and women. It's for anyone who recognizes that telling girls and young women to strive to lead provides a societal benefit to all of us, regardless of gender. This book is calling all moms, dads, grandmas, grandpas, aunts, uncles, bosses, and co-workers. It's a reminder that if we treat everyone as equals and recognize that women can aim high and should be in leadership, we can change the world.

1

IT'S BIGGER THAN COFFEE

Coffee is the fuel that powers the office. It keeps you going in between back-to-back meetings. It warms your hands on a cold winter's morning. It is the business travel companion that enables you to weather early morning or red-eye flights and time zone changes. It is the tonic that gets you through hump day. In many countries, coffee is sipped among friends while they relax and enjoy creative debate and conversation. However, for many professionals, especially in the U.S., coffee is practically funneled intravenously. Coffee represents productivity. Coffee matters.

When I started my career, I noticed someone would get sent out of the room to grab coffee for a client or other people who were considered important. It always seemed that the person who was sent—or even the one who offered–to get coffee happened to be a woman. One morning, a female vice president was asked to grab coffee for a group of male executives. In doing so, she missed out on the initial part of that meeting, which covered her subject-matter area. The VP had several key initiatives pending, but since she wasn't in the room, the men proceeded to make decisions on her

1

behalf. Because I was new in my career and still watching and learning, I noticed how men looked at the women who were being sent out for coffee. It became apparent that when they took on these administrative tasks, these women were viewed as having a lesser role in the company, regardless of their job title.

So let's get something straight. The point of this book isn't to start a movement in which professional women across the world stop getting coffee. There is always a time and a place to grab a cup for a colleague or a customer under the right circumstances. Rather, this book is about learning to unlearn. It is essential that we recognize the lifetime of training women in our culture receive. Girls are taught over and over again to be nice, patient, and polite, and women are expected to put their self-interests second because it's "the right thing to do."

The training starts while we are young. According to a study of 10,000 users from *BusyKid*,[5] a mobile app that tracks the weekly allowances given to children, among children between the ages of 5 and 7, boys make 50 percent more than girls. The study also indicates boys are more likely to be paid for showering or brushing their teeth, while girls often do these tasks with less or no incentive at all. Now, the solution is not to have our daughters go on strike by refusing to shower without being paid (regardless of how effective that might be) but, rather, for us to recognize how girls and women are often encouraged to take care of things *just because* and how this messaging can translate into the workplace.

---

[5] Paul, Kari. "The Wage Gap Starts at Home: Boys Are Paid More than Girls for Household Chores." *MarketWatch*, April 2, 2019. http://www.marketwatch.com/story/the-wage-gap-starts-at-home-boys-are-paid-more-than-girls-for-household-chores-2018-07-06. Accessed August 22, 2021.

During business meetings over dinner, I've noticed women piling the plates on top of each other and helping the busser clean the table. Bussing the table is clearly not their job, but many women seem to do it out of obligation or instinct. I'm not saying no one should be helpful in a work-related setting. If you are an administrative assistant, then securing coffee, ordering lunches, and getting the room ready can be a part of your job responsibilities. The question, however, is why so many women *in leadership* continue to do these tasks, even when they are not their responsibilities.

Asking a Woman to Take Notes Is the Modern Version of Asking a Woman to Get Coffee

Early on during the COVID-19 pandemic, I was invited to a number of invite-only calls for CEOs. During these strategy calls, I started to notice a trend. Every time we moved into breakout rooms or had brainstorming sessions, the organizer would unmute their line and ask the same question: "Will someone take notes?" Then they would stare into their camera and wait, hoping someone would raise their hand. As we sat there in silence, the majority of the time, the person who was eventually asked, or who volunteered, turned out to be a woman.

Now, they didn't volunteer quickly; but, too often, in a mixed group of men and women, one of the female CEOs would respond to the unseen pressure. Even when most of the CEOs were women, none of the men would volunteer. The unfortunate aspect of being the person who volunteers to take notes is that you often play a reduced role in the conversation. I found that was the case during these strategy calls.

It is essential that we provide a platform in which everyone feels compelled to participate in the conversation. Here are a few options to consider in the future:

- Work with the meeting organizer to have an assigned scribe for each call.
- Be conscious of the agenda and be aware of who is taking on what role.
- Have a calendar or sign-up sheet to make sure there are rotating scribes and/or roles.
- Create a note-taking template and make it accessible to all attendees. This will alleviate some of the pressure related to the organization of thoughts.

I remember those early days of the pandemic when we were all working to adjust to the new normal of a virtual environment. A large number of calls were centered on brainstorming and searching for the way forward when working with groups and meeting with people who were often together for the first time in that new setting. It was very reasonable to ask someone to take notes with no advance notice, but why was it always a woman who agreed to do so? This doesn't mean a woman should never take notes. But it should not be implied that it is a woman's responsibility to do an administrative task.

Now, you may believe the old mantra "if you want something done right, you have to do it yourself," but I want all of us to think about what happens when you agree to do an administrative task. For example, when you are taking notes, in some way or another, you are inherently silencing yourself. This doesn't mean the person who is taking notes can't contribute, but it does mean she can't dedicate her full attention to sharing her own thoughts because she has accepted the role of a scribe and is focused on writing down the thoughts of others.

The dilemma of taking notes relates to the overall theme of this book. *Never Get Their Coffee* is not simply about running errands or getting coffee. It's about how you act in a business environment and how the roles women take on affect the way they are seen and treated by others. *Never Get Their Coffee* is a metaphor for being aware of the pitfalls of putting women in stereotypically female roles. Sometimes, choosing not to volunteer for lesser roles can prompt an organization to take steps to prepare better in advance. If no one volunteers to get coffee, maybe management will set up a sign-up sheet or hire additional interns or admins. If no one volunteers to take notes, maybe group members will choose to take turns or use a random number generator to assign tasks. Women in leadership should not be expected to perform administrative tasks just because they are women, and they certainly should not put themselves in those types of situations voluntarily.

How to Have a Solution-Based Conversation

If your peers keep asking you to do work you feel is below your job responsibilities, first try to address the problem directly by pulling them aside and explaining the pattern you have noticed. It's always best to try to have those solution-based conversations in a smaller setting. While standing up and announcing your frustration in front of a room of twenty people may feel good in the moment, there's a more politically savvy way of addressing the situation. Share your thoughts in a one-on-one conversation and provide feedback on how you think that responsibility should be assigned in the future. Your peers may not even realize they have been operating from an unconscious bias. If the individual conversation doesn't work, you may have to escalate the issue and speak with your manager.

Here are some suggestions for initiating a solution-based conversation.

With Your Peers

- Address the problem directly.

- Try to have a one-on-one conversation.

- Keep the conversation light-hearted and social, if possible.

With Your Boss

- Have a solution in mind.

- Phrase your ideas as suggestions, not demands.

- Share your feelings but assume no ill-intent.

If your boss is the one who is asking you to do work that would normally be assigned to a position below yours, be patient and find a way to address it at the right time. I have found it's best to go into those conversations with the mindset that the other person did not have a negative intention when they made the request. Have the conversation in a more social environment when possible. Remember, everybody's human and we all make errors. Having a solution in mind prior to your conversation can be essential for alleviating frustration.

Sample Conversation

"I've noticed when we have meetings with all the directors, even though I'm a senior director, I'm the one who's always asked to take notes. The other directors are men and, in this situation, I feel like I'm being asked to take notes because I'm a woman. Taking notes is an administrative job, and if there is no admin available who can take notes for the group, I would appreciate it if each of us took turns at future meetings, so note-taking could become a shared responsibility of the team. Is this something you're amenable to?"

If your manager appears put off by your request, you may want to close your conversation by saying, "I'm sure there was no negative intention in assigning me that task. You've always been a supportive manager, so I thought it was important to let you know how it makes me feel and that I had noticed people had begun treating me differently."

These conversations can be difficult, but they are preferable to spending years feeling as if you are being looked down upon or given administrative tasks when something could be resolved with a simple conversation. It is important for your growth as a leader to be able to have conversations that take you out of your comfort zone. Verbal communication allows you to provide more nuanced insights into these topics and is preferable to written communication in these circumstances. If you are feeling anxiety and frustration related to how you are perceived, these feelings must be expressed in the proper setting, as they will not magically go away. Leadership is all about addressing challenges in a professional way and moving forward.

Summary

- Women leaders should be treated the same as their male counterparts.
- Notice who is being asked to do administrative tasks, such as taking notes and fetching coffee.
- Initiate solution-based conversations that help you focus on your overall goals.

How Motherhood Changed
Me—or Not

I've never not been a mother and a professional. My professional and maternal lives began in Mississippi. I graduated law school in the spring of 1986, passed the bar that summer, and started a prestigious clerkship with a federal judge in the fall. My first daughter was born in the summer of 1987 and the second in the spring of 1989. During the fall of 1988, I started work at a progressive law firm on a partnership track. My then-husband wisely never suggested that I should act more traditionally. He was the primary caregiver for our oldest daughter during her first year and became a teacher to accommodate our family life and because that was what he wanted.

For some reason, I didn't notice that the gender roles for women in the deep South were very conservative and traditional. Women were expected to choose between work and being wives and mothers. For a woman with my education and background, doing both was certainly not encouraged, and was frowned upon by many. That there might have been naysayers or risks didn't register with me. A law clerk who worked for another judge was fired for being pregnant. At the purportedly progressive law firm where I worked, one of the partners who was slightly older than me told me I could not expect to be a mother and a partner. Another partner made sexual passes at me. My mother asked tearful questions about how I felt being away from my babies.

I kept moving. Looking back over almost forty years in the professional world, I know there is power in not worrying about what other people with power and authority might think or do. You cannot control that. You can control what you do. You can do what you do with joy and integrity and a sense of purpose.

—Lindsay Coates, non-profit executive

2

YOU DESERVE IT, PLEASE STOP APOLOGIZING

In September 2018, I gave a presentation at the Women in Residential Construction conference with the dual title of "Learning to Unlearn/Please Stop Apologizing." This presentation was given three days after tennis pro Naomi Osaka beat Serena Williams at the U.S. Open to win her first-ever Grand Slam final. The match was awash with controversy after a referee penalized Williams for a game in the middle of the second set. At that point, Osaka was already leading and had proven her skill as she soundly won the match. I am sure, considering the controversy, that beating someone she looked up to and her age may have been factors in her response. However, it was still unfortunate that at Osaka's shining moment, she promptly apologized by saying, "I know that everyone was cheering for her [Serena]. I'm sorry it had to end like this."

It was an absolute shock for me to see Osaka achieve her lifelong dream at the highest level, and then immediately to begin apologizing for her success. I almost wanted to cry for her. Can you imagine an apology from Rafael Nadal in 2004 when he beat Roger Federer in straight sets? Nadel was only 17 years old but was excited about the win. Would you ever see a Super Bowl MVP apologize for winning, while simultaneously empathizing with the fans who rooted against him? Why couldn't Osaka be happy about this incredible accomplishment without feeling the need to apologize for defeating Williams, who holds the record for the most combined Open Era Grand Slam titles and is one of the most accomplished athletes in history? Osaka's apology reminded me of a recurring problem I'd seen in business: women have been taught that when you achieve something and everyone around you was expecting a different result, you should apologize for your success.

Osaka's apology made me think of why I was giving the presentation at the Women in Residential Construction conference in the first place. The conference from the previous year featured a Q&A at the end of a session in which a young woman stood up and questioned whether it made sense for women who worked in the residential construction industry to have a conference if men were not also in attendance. I quickly responded with the observation that a group of men would never question the importance of their lunch, happy hour, or meeting if there were no women in attendance.

During my presentation about learning to unlearn, I discussed the staggering statistics that showcase the small number of women in the industry. The share of women in all occupations combined as of 2013 was 47.2 percent; but in the construction industry, women only made up 2.6 percent of the workforce.[6] I stressed the importance of women

---

[6] "Employed Persons by Detailed Industry, Sex, Race, and Hispanic or Latino Ethnicity." U.S. Bureau of Labor Statistics. January 22, 2021. https://www.bls.gov/cps/cpsaat18.htm. Accessed August 22, 2021.

not only entering the industry but also the critical need to highlight and celebrate women in leadership positions. For other women to want to enter a field, they need to see there is a place for them and room to grow. I reminded the audience that women need to lead. I also pointed out that even though women may have different approaches and styles to leadership, we should embrace our uniqueness because it is an asset. For example, women often have a servant leadership style and an empathetic approach and are more proactive than reactive as managers.

Of course, a key message I always like to enforce is for women to please stop apologizing. I gave a few examples of unnecessary apologies and then allowed the group to discuss their own experiences.

Needless to say, the topic of apologizing was a hot one at the Women in Residential Construction conference. Everyone has many examples to share once you bring up the issue. This conference was no different, and great discussions took place during the group breakouts.

Other key tips I shared with the women at the event included the following:

- **Effective leaders are confident.**
  Be sure to trust in yourself as a leader. Your opinion and ideas matter. Believe in yourself and show that you do so through your words.
- **Accept feedback.**
  Sometimes people offer us feedback that could be seen as negative. Before you respond, listen and process what was said to you. Don't take everything so personally.
  Use negative feedback to improve the customer experience.
  The greater our ability to accept feedback, the greater our capacity to grow and succeed.

- **Use your passion as your strength**.
  Part of what makes a woman a great leader is her compassion. You can show your concern and care for your employees, your company, and your bottom line, all while remaining a strong and self-assured leader.

My presentation was the first thing in the morning and after the lunch break another speaker named Elitia took the stage. Elitia chose to share a very personal story of her struggle in the industry and what she experienced as a woman of color. She opened up by showing a video clip of the very powerful scene from the TV series *Scandal* in which Olivia Pope and her father are arguing about decisions she's made in life. He reminds her of a message he'd told her over and over again as she was growing up. He said, "You have to be twice as good as them to get half of what they have."

Elitia shared that her father had given her that same message growing up. It was an emotional memory, and she began to tear up. She then apologized for the tears and everyone shouted, "Please don't apologize!" Ugh! Okay, so that was the moment I wanted to crawl under the table. There are times when it's okay to apologize. If someone agrees to share an emotional moment in their life to reinforce their message, let them. It is important for us to understand the trials and tribulations they went through to get where they are today. I had started the day by giving a speech about not apologizing and ended the day apologizing to the speaker for that uncomfortable moment. In the end, we must assess each situation and always support each other as women leaders.

The next day, I spoke with a woman named Suzanne, who had been working for thirty years in residential construction. She expressed that early in her career, she had been pulled aside and told: "When you raise your hand in a meeting or offer your input, be sure to begin with the words, 'with all due respect.'" This quickly became a habit Suzanne developed while sitting in countless meetings that were primarily full of men. She was taught to provide a *de facto* apology simply for having an opinion about her job. Suzanne said she was preparing to retire and had recently trained a new employee who was in her twenties and had given the young woman that same advice. She did not recognize that she was training another generation of apologizers. After our discussion, she was energized and said that offering different advice to that employee would be the first thing she'd do when she got back into the office.

The good news is, this epidemic of apologizing is something we can fix through recognition and awareness. If those techniques don't work, there are technological solutions, such as phone applications and Google's Just Not Sorry browser plug-in, which warns you to stop apologizing so much in Gmail. The fact that deferring to others has become so ingrained into our communication that we'd need technology to assist demonstrates the scale of the problem.

"Men are taught to apologize for their weaknesses,
women for their strengths."
—*Lois Wyse, Author*

Bestselling Author Lois Wyse was an advertising pioneer and businesswoman who rose through the ranks in the *Mad Men* era of the '50s, '60s, and '70s. Like so many, she paved the way for the next generation by fighting for her seat at the table. Her quote has gained a renewed focus in the post-#MeToo era, and it stands as relevant as ever. While many readers focus on the contrast between weakness and strength, I ask you to take another look at Wyse's quote and think about the importance of the words "are taught." The next generation of leaders should not live in fear of displaying their strengths, but the same is also true for weakness. A leader should not shy away from seeking help, partnering with a team, or taking a moment to breathe when the stress of the job can seem overwhelming. Sometimes acknowledging moments of vulnerability without feeling the need to apologize is critical for mental health. In other words, men being taught to apologize for weakness is a problem, too.

Do Not Fall into the Uncertainty Trap

Several years back, my former company sent all senior staff to the Center for Creative Leadership for an executive development program. I was excited about the opportunity to get 360-degree feedback from my peers and employees and compare their input to the way I viewed myself. During this training, they covered a variety of topics, but the part I found most interesting was my one-on-one time with the coach, during which we discussed the results of my 360 feedback exercise. I personally was shocked to hear my lowest rating didn't come from my boss, my employees, or my peers, but rather from myself. The coach spent most of her time telling me I should have more confidence in myself because I had the talent to lead my own organization. This was many years before I became a CEO. It was a reminder that the only person holding me back was me.

When you are speaking in a meeting or giving a pitch, do not waste energy searching for head nods, smiles, or non-verbal cues from others. Your search for validation is noticeable and may come across as weak. Let's remind ourselves of Dr. Albert Mehrabian's 7-38-55 Rule of Personal Communication, which says that words represent only 7 percent of communication while body language (55 percent) and tone of voice (38 percent) make up the remaining 93 percent.[7] This is one of the most widely cited studies in the field of communication. If you're like me, you've probably heard this study repeated over and over in classrooms, meetings, and conferences. However, until I started my research for this book, I never realized that Dr. Mehrabian's 1967 study tested only inconsistent messages. If there's one thing we know for sure, you must believe in your words for them to have weight and power. When you are uncertain, your heart beats faster, you might begin to sweat, and your facial expressions will give you away. If you believe in what you are saying and think confidently, your non-verbal cues will follow suit.

It is important for women to recognize their internal power. We must stop analyzing our flaws and start declaring our strengths. It is time for us to stand confidently by our decisions and ideas without worrying about how that makes others feel. We should practice not harping on simple mistakes and recognize that every flaw can be a gateway to growth. This is a future in which we build each other up one moment at a time. And in that future, we all benefit.

Sample Conversations

Below are some examples of the sample conversations I shared at the Women in Residential Construction conference to showcase unnecessary apologies.

Example #1

Sally had a client scheduled to visit the office and meet with a few other members of her team. The client's flight

---

[7] Harrison, Kim. "Ignore This Big 55%-38%-7% Nonverbal Communication Myth." *Cutting Edge PR Insights*, June 1, 2020. http://www.cuttingedgepr.com/ignore-big-55-38-7-nonverbal-communication-myth/. Accessed August 22, 2021.

is late and now the meeting needs to be pushed back. Sally hears of the flight delay and sends the following email to her colleagues:

"I'm sorry, but my client's flight is delayed. Do you mind moving the 9 a.m. meeting to 10 a.m.? Thanks for your understanding and I'm sorry for the inconvenience."

Question: Did Sally actually cause the flight delay? Did she fiddle with the landing gear or reach up to the heavens and create bad weather conditions? If not, why is she apologizing?

Here is an example of a more appropriate email from Sally:

"Hello. My client's flight is delayed. I need to move the meeting from 9 a.m. to 10 a.m. Let me know if you are not available at that time. Thank you."

Sally will still provide the same information, but without the unnecessary apology.

Example #2

Here is another example I have often seen or heard:

Renee just completed a communications report, and it needs to be edited. She sends an email to Roger, the editor on staff, and it reads as follows:

"I'm sorry to bother you, Roger, but would you mind editing the attached report for me before I send it out?"

Question: Is Roger a paid editor? If so, why is it a bother for you to ask him to do his job? And again, why apologize for asking someone to do their job? They get paid to do their job.

Here is an example of a more appropriate email from Renee:

"Hello, Roger. Attached is the latest communications report in need of an edit. Let me know when you will be able to complete the edit and if you have any questions. Thank you."

Summary

- Celebrate your success; don't apologize for it.
- Avoid unnecessary apologies in the workplace.
- Highlight the accomplishments of other women.
- Effective leaders are confident. It shows in your positive body language, decisiveness, and belief in yourself.
- Use your passion as your strength. A charismatic and innovative leader is someone people want to follow and support.

Learn to Be Gangster

Learn to be gangster! That is the reminder I set up on my phone the day I realized being nice wasn't going to help. I am an educated woman with a unique skill set. I found that, in order to move forward, it wasn't about what I could offer but how I wrapped the package.

I started inviting myself to join various work projects. I exposed myself to numerous leaders across my organization. Most importantly, I stopped asking for permission or waiting for someone to invite me to a certain group. I created a plan of action and value proposition statement. This allowed me to share my knowledge and gain exposure to a variety of leaders who were paying attention. My reputation began to grow as a person who gets things done. Someone who can manage a project well while maintaining a positive and upbeat attitude. This started to catch on and strengthened my brand within my organization. My shift in behavior truly opened up additional paths for advancement.

—Jennifer L. Downs, M.B.A., healthcare business development leader

3

I AM WHO YOU MADE ME

I recently served as a speaker at Women in Leadership town hall. During the discussion, a panelist referenced the famous Howard and Heidi case study, which revealed that gender bias can happen when comparing fictional resumes that are identical except for the name. We talked about the results of the study and how Heidi was judged harshly and considered unlikeable despite having professional accomplishments that were no different from Howard's. After the town hall, a young professional posted in the chat and asked, "What are women supposed to do to get ahead?"

In the past, I have given advice to many professionals, both younger and older, who would ask me to lunch or coffee to seek specific guidance or strategies for their own professional growth. My number one recommendation is to channel your inner confidence. I stand by that advice, but I can see why so many women struggle with confidence in a world where you face a negative reaction from nearly any choice you make.

- When you exhibit *confidence*, they take it as *bossy*.

- When you are more *generous* and *giving*, you're considered *weak*.
- When you have a new idea, people focus on how it can *fail* instead of on how it can *succeed*.

Not long ago, at a committee meeting, I noticed the female presenter gave more attention and appeared to direct all her comments to the men on the committee. In addition, those men, some of whom had worked with her previously, also dominated the conversation. There were other women and minorities on the committee, including myself. As we listened, it felt like we were peering in on a conversation between an old boys' club and a former protégé. As I think back on the experience, I truly believe the woman was exactly what I'm defining by the phrase "I am what you made me." I am sure that to get to where she was in her career, she had to conform to the mindset of men and adapt to their mentality. She may not have even noticed the implicit bias shown to the women and minorities in the room because she had been taught to focus on the older white men. Many women have experienced a lifetime of working with all white male decision-makers and, therefore, why would they focus on anyone other than the group who determined their financial future?

A friend of mine recently shared an informative TED Talk by Dana Kanze called "The Real Reason Female Entrepreneurs Get Less Funding."[8] The talk dives into why women own 39 percent of all businesses in the U.S. but get only 2.3 percent of venture funding.[9] Kanze reviewed nearly 2,000 questions asked during presentations and

[8] Kanze, Dana. "The Real Reason Female Entrepreneurs Get Less Funding." *TED Talks*, December 20, 2018. https://www.ted.com/talks/dana_kanze_the_real_reason_female_entrepreneurs_get_less_funding.

[9] Bittner, Ashley, and Brigette Lau. "Women-Led Startups Received Just 2.3% of VC Funding in 2020." *Harvard Business Review*, February 25, 2021. https://www.hbr.org/2021/02/women-

found a whopping 67 percent of the questions posed to male entrepreneurs were promotion focused while 66 percent of those posed to female entrepreneurs were prevention focused. In other words, venture capitalists (VCs) were offering men chances to talk about how their money could grow while questioning women about how their money could stay safe.

According to the *MIT Technology Review*, 65 percent of venture capital firms have no female partners and 81 percent have no Black investors.[10] According to the website Allraise.org, women occupy only 12 percent of the decision-maker roles at large U.S.-based venture capital firms.[11] When you review this data in conjunction with Kanze's finding about gender bias in VC presentations, it truly puts a spotlight on how we address each other. So many of us grow up being told to "look to the stars." But if some are asked to "reach higher" while others are told to "be careful of falling," we may not experience the same velocity at liftoff.

Women As Equals When Not Seen Equally

In a previous job, I was often left out of meetings during which the topic being discussed was directly related to my job responsibilities and my team. I'm sure many people

---

led-startups-received-just-2-3-of-vc-funding-in-2020. Accessed August 22, 2021.

[10] Roush, Wade. "Podcast: Lassoing the Venture Capital Cowboys." *MIT Technology Review*, July 15, 2020. http://www.technologyreview.com/2020/07/15/1005192/podcast-lassoing-the-venture-capital-cowboys/. Accessed August 22, 2021.

[11] Kostka, Pam. "More Women Became VC Partners Than Ever Before in 2019." *Medium*, All Raise, February 14, 2020. http://www.medium.com/allraise/more-women-became-vc-partners-than-ever-before-in-2019-39cc6cb86955. Accessed August 22, 2021.

would think this does not happen in this day and age, but women still need to fight for their right to sit at the table and simply do their job. It is a continuous struggle. When I discovered I was not included in those meetings, I asked why and received a thinly veiled list of reasons. My boss soon agreed I needed to attend the meeting but tried to exclude me from the social events that followed. Some went so far as to assume they were saving me from having to attend a sporting event, even though I'm a big sports fan. Assuming someone would not like a certain activity based on gender demonstrates the importance of changing company culture from the top and focusing on equity in your Diversity Equity and Inclusion (DEI) training. It is critical that we have leaders at the top of an organization who focus on DEI and are intentional about their efforts. Diversity training will help companies avoid these unnecessary and unacceptable situations in the future.

Another troubling experience involved a former boss who declined to travel with me to a customer meeting unless another man in the organization was also included. My boss said he was not comfortable traveling alone with a female employee. He designated a male co-worker to join us, even though the other man had no responsibility or role in these client meetings. I recognize in the era of the #MeToo movement that some men may feel the need to be extra cautious in the workplace. However, we must recognize that having one-on-one time with leadership outside of the office is often essential for people to grow in their executive positions. If only men are invited on a golf trip, then those men will have an undue advantage over the women on staff. Please remember, the #MeToo movement doesn't mean men can't talk to women—just that men shouldn't sexually assault them. If someone can't tell the difference, you should question whether that person is a right fit for a leadership role.

Societal Impact May Affect a Woman's Ability to Grow in Her Career

When I was still dating, men often had an issue if they found out my job title was more impressive than theirs. Consequently, I tried to dumb down what I did for a living. Instead of saying I was a director, I would say, "I do marketing stuff." In a casual setting, some of the men I worked with told me I wouldn't find a husband because I wasn't needy enough and that men needed to feel like providers. I would reply by saying, "They can provide me with love, affection, support and a whole host of other relationship needs." This helpful insight was echoed by my male friends who agreed that I could certainly find dates, but no one would want to settle down with a successful girl. As time passed, I continued to read articles such as the 2013 study from the University of Chicago, which found that having a wife who earns more than the husband increases the likelihood of divorce by fifty percent.[12] The data coincidentally came out the same year I married my wonderful husband.

As I told my social circle about my early dating struggles, I recall one of my guy friends eyeballing the floor, shrugging his shoulders, and saying, "Maybe you can't always have it all." Time and again, as I progressed in my career, both men and women would often ask whether women could have it all. It made me realize over time that a woman should never have to debate whether her professional growth would lead to personal stagnation. It's up to all of us to prepare a fair and more equitable world, and to demonstrate to each other that our destiny is not tied to external perceptions.

---

[12] Lambert, Emily. "When Women Earn More Than Their Husbands." *The University of Chicago Booth School of Business*, February 18, 2013. http://www.chicagobooth.edu/media-relations-and-communications/press-releases/when-women-earn-more-than-their-husbands. Accessed August 22, 2021.

The Heart of the Issue

Over half the graduates of culinary school are women, but less than seven percent of restaurants are owned by women.
—*Susan Ungaro, President, James Beard Foundation*

According to research from LeanIn.org and McKinsey, the biggest obstacle for women occurs at one of the very first steps on the corporate ladder, which is the initial promotion to management.[13] The study determined that men are far more likely to be promoted from their entry-level jobs to management and stated that for every 100 men promoted and hired to Manager, only 72 women are promoted and hired. The report continues, outlining that since men outnumber women at the manager level, "[t]here are significantly fewer women to hire or promote to senior managers. The number of women decreases at every subsequent level." The study refers to this as the "broken rung."

If we go back to Kanze's TED Talk and dive into the data, it shows that VCs displayed the same implicit bias regardless of their gender. Female VCs asked male entrepreneurs promotion questions and then turned around and asked female entrepreneurs prevention questions. The female VCs operated just like their male counterparts.

The key is to focus on what makes you unique and leverage your creativity, insight, and focus using a results-driven perspective. We, as men and women, must not fall into the traps of trying to play the part of traditional social roles at the expense of our authentic selves. It takes all of us to complete the puzzle of success by bringing together a variety of different people and perspectives.

---

[13] "Women in the Workplace 2019." McKinsey & Company. https://womenintheworkplace.com/2019. Accessed August 22, 2021.

Women must be champions for other women. I still see examples time and time again of women in leadership roles who fail to elevate women. I attended a leadership conference for female CEOs, led by a female keynote speaker. The purpose of this event was to promote women and elevate their image, stature, and mindset as leaders. During one section of the session, the speaker showcased a video of what she referred to as exceptional leadership from which we could all learn. I was eagerly anticipating which female leader she would highlight, but instead it was a man.

Women already face so many struggles to achieve leadership. It is important that we celebrate those who have made it and listen to their strategic vision and messages of hope. I don't blame the keynote speaker. I'm sure she was trained to look toward men for examples of great leadership. But that is why I want to stress the importance of being intentional in lifting up, showcasing, and celebrating women as leaders.

How many exceptional women leaders can you think of right now? How many female executives have been elevated to those roles through struggle and determination? How diverse is the list of leaders you are thinking of right now? Not only do we need to think of great female leaders who look like us, but we must also continue to educate ourselves about the long list of diverse women who are excelling in a variety of fields. The numbers are often small, depending on the industry, but we should seek them out and learn from all of their experiences. We have a lot of work to do if we plan to ingrain in the minds of both men and women that women also have great vision and we should look toward female leaders equally.

Don't Let Doubt Become Your Default

As I prepared to write this book, I spoke with a number of female CEOs about their journey to success and found a common thread. So many of them were constantly second-guessed in their decisions, regardless of the scope of gravity of their ideas. I'm not talking about the normal vetting process that takes place in every business, but rather, a prevalent level of questioning that was directed toward these women, regardless of how minor the impact of their ideas might be on the business. One woman in my professional network said, "There was a point in my career when I started to dread the scrutiny that came with being the only female leader in the room. However, I soon realized the alternative was not to be there at all." Her insight was important. Because while fighting through scrutiny and second-guessing can be stressful, we have to remember that if we let it drag us down, the alternative is not being in the room at all. I think the sad result of this questioning process is that we begin to internalize it. When the time comes to share a thought or sit at the table, we are so busy having a debate within our own heads that we may stay silent and miss our opportunity to shine.

Successful leaders have the strength to move forward confidently regardless of whether their ideas are popular. Many of us are so focused on being liked in the workplace that it can hinder our opportunities for growth. If your primary goal is to appease others, you will fall into the trap of maintaining the status quo and allowing others to control the narrative, even when you disagree. When you complete a project successfully, write a report that highlights your achievements and have those results ready the next time you have to back up a tough decision within the never-ending wheel of scrutiny. The reality is, being likeable is not always part of the path to becoming a leader. It is essential that we stop trying to mimic the traits of others and embrace our true authentic selves.

Recently, I was on a call with several women in leadership and one woman (I'll refer to her as Donna) raised four separate issues she experienced in her career. I believe many of the issues she brought up have been experienced by other women in leadership. It is important to review these points and think if any of these challenges are applicable.

Women Against Other Women

So often, executive boards and leadership teams significantly lack female representation. When a woman grows up in a world in which there is *only one* promotion or *only one* shot at getting into the boys' club, it's easy for her to form the habit of seeing other successful females who could potentially take her place as a threat. Instead of taking this woman under your wing and choosing to mentor her, you may try to avoid putting her in a role in which she could take your place among the limited number of positions in the hierarchy. People often joke about how some women can't seem to get along, but if a woman has grown up with the perception that spaces for women are limited, she may try incredibly hard to conform and potentially clash with other women. This has been the reality of the workforce for many generations. It is changing but, for some, these old habits are dying hard. We need to partner together to lead to transformative change so we can do away with token female executives and make female executives become the norm.

Generational Changes

Donna was an alumna of the U.S. Naval Academy. When she went back for a reunion, she was surprised to hear the feedback from the women in the academy today. Donna said, "When I was there, we used to complain that we were only eight percent of the Academy and we needed to grow. Now they complain they're only thirty percent and they still think we need to grow. So some things did change over the last generation."

Race

Donna noted it was tough enough to be a woman in leadership, but her African American friend has it much harder in the work environment. Donna said, "To be a woman and a minority is a far different experience. To make matters worse, my friend is in her childbearing years, so it is a triple whammy."

Childbearing

A thought-provoking video by McKinsey & Company known as "Addressing Unconscious Bias" takes a male professional through the microaggressions, snide comments, and challenges many women experience in the workplace.[14] One truly eye-opening example was when the boss asked the man if he'd like to switch to part-time and forgo a promotion now that a baby was on the way. So much of our unconscious bias ties back to the way people, both male and female, treat women who want to have a family.

At the end of the session, the big takeaways from that day were centered around the knowledge sharing that Donna provided. Other women on the call felt free to share when they may have been the woman holding another woman back. The overall message was that it is important

---

[14] "Addressing Unconscious Bias." McKinsey & Company. *YouTube*, May 12, 2016. https://www.youtube.com/watch?v=O8UIW_Pi5wU. Accessed August 22, 2021.

to continue to talk about these issues so that we are more aware of ongoing bias in the workplace and strive to end it.

Lesson for Young Women: Never Let Your Worth Be Defined by Someone Else

All across the world, the fear of public speaking is consistently ranked as people's number-one fear. I wonder how much of that self-doubt begins as a result of the negative thoughts, comments, and interactions we face while growing up. Each time we speak, we may remember the moments when someone made a face on the playground or judged us by whispering in the back of the classroom. I wonder how many of our friends and family choose not to start a business, share quality ideas, or put themselves in new situations because of the fear of being judged.

"You may encounter many defeats, but you must not be defeated."
— Maya Angelou

I am not advocating that everyone should go through life without facing any challenges. Messing around, playing jokes, and yes, even hurling insults are certainly part of life. But I never want to see another young woman hesitate to share her voice publicly because she feels the risk of being judged by their peers is too great. We have to stop making it so easy to tear each other down and encourage the next generation to never feel defeated by the words and actions of others.

The way the world is:

- Women are judged based on their looks at a much higher rate than men.

The way the world should be:

- Women and men should be judged equally.

Every day, young girls are led to believe they must look pretty and be nice to be valued. They are given social cues that teach them female worth is measured by these two things above all else.

Often, the insults women face can be summarized in five words:

- I don't think you're pretty.
- I don't think you're nice.

I want the next generation to understand these insults are cloaked in the belief that young women should strive to look pretty and act nice most of the time. But the reality is that effective leaders have moments when they can't be nice. When you are delivering hard data or less than ideal survey results, your appearance and tone should not be bubbly. How many salary negotiations have ended with lower pay because a woman didn't want to rock the boat? How many times have women been passed over for a promotion because they wanted to be team players? As compared to boys, how much more often are girls told to hold back or be careful during their lifetime?

So many women face harassment and societal pressure to smile. We are training generation after generation to have unfair expectations of themselves, from the t-shirts and outfits we dress girls in, to the neighbors and strangers who begin conversations with young girls by commenting on their looks. One of the most profound commentaries

I've seen on this subject was a viral video in which an eight-year-old girl reviews the T-shirts at a department store.

She notices the girl's t-shirts have slogans such as these:

- Hey!
- Beautiful
- I feel fabulous

While the boy's T-shirts say:

- Think outside the box
- Hero
- Let's explore!

These T-shirts are reflecting the idea that men should be judged primarily by their actions, and that girls should be judged primarily based on appearance. The TED Talk "To Raise Brave Girls, Encourage Adventure" by Caroline Paul makes an intriguing point about how we socialize young girls as compared to young boys. Caroline says, "...at this young age, girls and boys are actually very alike physically. In fact, girls are often stronger until puberty, and more mature. And yet we adults act as if girls are more fragile and more in need of help, and they can't handle as much."[15]

When I was growing up, I also noticed that many of my male peers were encouraged to explore and try new things, while so many of my female peers were encouraged to play it safe. I make it a point to provide high expectations for the career women I mentor and set that same example for my daughter.

---

[15] Paul, Caroline. "To Raise Brave Girls, Encourage Adventure." *TED Talks*, October 15, 2016. https://www.ted.com/talks/caroline_paul_to_raise_brave_girls_encourage_adventure. Accessed August 22, 2021.

My husband is an educator at a middle school in Washington, D.C. A few years ago, he was serving as the assistant girls' volleyball coach. At the beginning of the season, he noticed many of the girls would play in a manner he described as "polite." They would *defer* or allow their teammates to get the ball, which often resulted in two motionless girls watching the ball hit the ground.

After losing three of their first four games, he spent an entire practice doing one specific drill. He tossed the ball in the air and made the girls shout "I got it!" over and over again, as loudly as possible. He found the volleyball team only got better when the girls finally accepted they had to *demand* and *own* their space on the court. After my husband instilled that drill during practice, the team went undefeated for the remainder of the season and made the playoffs.

How many of our young girls are socialized to defer to others, even when they have tremendous talent and ability? So many of history's most impactful people were thinkers and adventures who left a memorable impression on the world because they believed in themselves. This spirit of adventure has shaped major breakthroughs across all industries, yet we create t-shirts with slogans that encourage only half of our population to be adventurous.

We cannot allow young women in society to believe the overwhelming majority of their self-worth is tied specifically to looks because it is a near-certainty that each will encounter at least one person who doesn't think she's pretty. We live in fear of being judged, but the criteria by which we are judged are constantly changing. One month, the magazine covers are featuring thigh gaps. The next month, magazines are talking about how being curvy is in style. If we continue to live in fear of negative comments based on our looks, then we are setting ourselves up for failure.

It is important to shape your own path and lead in the way you feel is best. Find what matters in your life and shape your own sense of self-worth. Don't let others shape it for you.

Summary

- Women should assess whether they are exhibiting bias towards other women and correct that bias.
- We must work together to raise awareness of gender bias among venture capitalists so female leaders are given equal consideration.
- Women must be invited to participate and be given equal opportunities for growth.
- We must improve access for minority women in leadership positions.
- Equity for women in leadership requires both men and women to encourage and support that elevation.
- Women must be ready to demand their own space rather than waiting for opportunities to be presented to them.

Be Better to Each Other

On my first day back from my too-brief maternity leave, I walked into my academic staff meeting with my still-tender c-section bandaged and cinched into a compression belt. It was the last meeting of the day and my mind was heavy from a day of loaded questions from colleagues: "What about the baby? Are you thinking of staying home?" "How will you manage work-life balance?" And the most ridiculous, well-meaning comment of all: "Don't worry, you'll lose that baby weight in no time!" It was bad. There were breast milk jokes. I stood in the hallway to gather myself and overheard two people talking about me in a friendly, tsk-tsking way. They were talking about my body's "pregnancy bounce back" and expressing concern about how I would now juggle my family and career. I was rescued by the sound of a third voice interrupting, "Why are we even talking about this? She's great. I'm *so* glad to have her back!" In that moment, I felt grateful and strong and supported.

We've all had moments like this. We need people to speak up in support, solidarity, or just to shut down inappropriate chatter. As an interesting aside, my husband, on his first day back in the office had—you guessed it—zero discussion of how his new familial responsibilities might affect his work-life balance. They told him: "Congratulations on the baby! Glad you're back. Man, have we got work for you!"

In nearly twenty years of work in academia, I have come to understand that it takes one person to begin using their power to shut down often well-intentioned (but still toxic) assumptions directed towards women and women's bodies. We need to find the courage to be that person who speaks up to stop destructive practices, while actively making room for major positive changes to our workplace ideologies. We can, we will, and we must be better to each other. It's time.

—Adena Rojas, Former Senior Academic Program Coordinator, Department of Environmental Health and Engineering at Johns Hopkins University Whiting School of Engineering

THE DIRTY
SECRET: IMAGE *IS*
EVERYTHING

Sometimes we avoid the harsh reality, but the truth needs to be said even though it may hurt: Your appearance affects your career path. This is the uncomfortable, dirty little secret of business. The old phrase "dress for the job you want, not for the job you have" still applies today, at least in traditional corporate settings. When you are thinking about that promotion, you have to step inside the mind of the customer and other executives at your company.

Customer: If you can't even manage your appearance, how would you manage my account?

Executive: If you can't give yourself a professional image, how can you represent our company as a professional?

We have to face the fact that competition is more than what you know or who you know. A key part of competition is that your professional image can often make or break your career in an ever-changing and modern business environment. People who wear the same suit they've had for decades give others the impression they may be set in their ways and will approach business in the same way. The wear and tear on your clothing shows, and if you think that suit is a classic, you need to consider changing with the times.

Reality Check

Take care of yourself. Make sure you are well groomed, eat healthy, get your exercise, and, if you're a woman, don't be afraid to put on a little make-up. If you want to run a company, remember that you are the spokesperson and the face of the company. Trust me, I look forward to the day when people will be judged solely by their knowledge rather than their physical characteristics; but while I'm waiting, I'll be on the elliptical.

Image Tips to Keep in Mind
- Dress for your shape.
- Dress for your age.
- Keep up with current trends.

Professional Hair and Bias

Now, I mentioned above that in order to dress professionally, you must make sure your hair is well groomed. It is also important for executives to understand there are various looks for professional hair based on race. Often, leaders at companies are white males who do not know what types of hairstyles are considered appropriate for professional for women or men of varying races. In addition, women and men in the Black community continue to face challenges with various hairstyles being accepted.

The CROWN Act stands for Creating a Respectful and Open World for Natural Hair. It was created in 2019 to ensure protection against discrimination based on race-based hairstyles.[16] People should feel comfortable expanding their knowledge of other cultures and this includes gaining a better understanding of the variety of hairstyles that are appropriate in a professional environment. Don't automatically think that certain hairstyles aren't professional. Now, don't get me wrong... messed-up hair can happen to any person of any race. But because there can often be a bias against Black hairstyles in professional environments, some people feel they must avoid wearing a well-kept natural hairstyle that suits their personal preferences.

One thing is for certain: anyone, regardless of race or gender, can have messy hair. But also, everyone, no matter their race or gender, can wear their hair styled in a variety of ways and still look professional. Some people may choose to wear a professional head covering to work, it depends on their nationality, religion, or culture. The more businessmen and businesswomen broaden their understanding of what professional hairstyles look like for various races, the less bias people who work in corporate environments will show toward a potential employee, client, or employer.

Sesame Street introduced a new character named Segi. When the writer Joey Mazzarino was interviewed on CNN, he shared his story. He was inspired to write the song "I Love My Hair" because of his daughter whom he and his wife had adopted from Ethiopia. At four years old, she began to question her hair and wanted it to be straight or blonde. That's when Joey and his wife realized their daughter's hair was an issue, and they wanted her to love herself just as she is. Acceptance is central to improving confidence in our

---

[16] The Official CROWN Act. https://www.thecrownact.com/about. Accessed August 22, 2021.

image, and confidence in our image affects our confidence in our work.

"As First Lady, I was slowly watching myself being exposed to the world. I had to become more strategic in how I presented myself because it had the potential of defining me for the rest of my life. Fashion for a woman still predominates how people view you and that's not fair, that's not right, but it's true. And that's when fashion, isn't just fashion; it's how you turn into your tool, rather than being a victim of it..."
—Michelle Obama

This is a great topic to address with a trusted network of industry professionals. If you aren't already a part of a professional lunch or coffee group, consider creating one. We have to rely on each other to follow the trends and ask those nagging questions that are constantly running through our mind. It's better to spend a few minutes chatting with a close confidante than to spend a week doubting your professional dress choices.

Don't just declutter your closet, do some spring cleaning for your mind. I have heard both male and female friends ask for feedback regarding an outfit or new haircut before a big job interview. How many of us wake up, look at ourselves in the mirror, identify our flaws, and doubt our wardrobe choice right before an important sales pitch or client meeting? When you do this, your shoulders will slump, you will frown, hesitate before you speak, and say filler words like "um." Lastly, you will defer to others in the room who appear more confident and allow them to step in and drive the agenda. You must declutter your mind from all the negative comments and thoughts you've been holding onto for all these years. Do this by surrounding yourself with people who support you and whom you trust to give you feedback. And sometimes as women, you need the person in your life to whom you can text a picture of two outfits and help you choose the right one, or to FaceTime with as you spin around and hear them say, "You look good!"

So many of us replay a single negative comment over and over in our minds for days, weeks, and sometimes years. Just like they say in sports after an error, the best athletes have a short memory. If someone gives you negative feedback that tears you down, you need the person who can remind you of your inner strength, which can build you back up. You also need the person who can tell you the truth, but at the appropriate time.

When you receive criticism, do not withdraw and reflect over and over on the opinion of one person. Image is not solely what you wear on the outside; it is also how you feel about yourself on the inside. When I was younger, I was in pageants. The first time I entered a pageant, it was because my friend Jill was entering and I wanted to spend time with her. During the pageant, I was a classic teenager thinking about how much my feet hurt in those heels. In addition, my sportswear outfit was not some custom-made, cute, fitted top and shorts set, like so many girls wore. I thought they literally meant sports, so I wore my father's Washington Redskins sweatpants and sweatshirt and rolled up the arms and legs to fit. I strutted with pride in my tennis shoes and was in it for the fun.

I was shocked when I made it to the top ten. To me, that was a winning result for my first pageant. In the final round, we all went back out on stage to hear the names announced. As I clapped for the third runner up and then the second runner up, I was trying to ignore the pain in my aching feet. Then they announced the winner of Miss Teen Washington... and it was me! I clapped, looking around, and I had no idea they were talking about me. I was still focused on the pain in my feet. But once the girls said, "Hey, that's you!" the pain in my feet instantly went away and I was waving to my family.

Being in that pageant set a different course for me and my future. After that night, I realized I probably should practice wearing heels, but also that my personality and presence were important characteristics that could help me move forward in life.

I later went on to run the Ms. Petite Maryland International Pageant while I was in college. What I loved was that I discovered so many women who had inner beauty and such potential to flourish with their external image. During the pageant process, we taught interview skills, dressing for business, and preparing the young women for a future beyond this one pageant weekend. It was preparing them for the workforce that they were either already in or facing.

I would receive phone calls at midnight from girls asking questions about whether they should lose weight, if the clothes they already had would look good enough for the event, or if they should borrow money to buy something more expensive. I was in college when I first started running this pageant and it was an eye-opening experience for me, having been blessed with a mother and father who gave me all the advice these girls were asking me for. I was a 19-year-old girl offering feedback to ladies between the ages of 18 and 29 who truly did not know what they should do. So, I told them it's not about the dollars you spend; it's about making wise decisions with what you have available to you.

These young women were lovely, but many of them told me they had never had a mentor to consult about what constitutes professional dress or how to answer interview questions. How many professional women have that discerning friend or family member who can guide them in the right direction, help them with their wardrobe selection, and recognize what colors and styles look best for their shape?

There are so many unfair biases, from the employee who's so beautiful that many of her co-workers assume she was hired for her looks, despite her exceptional qualifications, to the person who's judged by their weight and not their knowledge. Even though some of these things are beyond our control, it's even more important we focus on the things we can control. People should just love you for who you are, but if you want to run a company and be a member of the C-suite, you must remember that all the decisions you make affect your future in a traditional business environment.

Our Virtual Image

The COVID-19 pandemic changed the economy for the foreseeable future and made remote work a staple of our lives. This means our appearance on a video chat may vary between friends, family, coworkers, and management. But as more work is conducted using this method, we should all take a moment to look at how we can improve that experience and demonstrate our credibility online.

- **Balance your image**. Learn how to distance yourself from the camera. If your laptop camera is located at the bottom of the screen, you may need to place the laptop on top of a few books, so we are not looking at your neck and chest instead of your face.

- **Check your resting face**. Practice in a mirror so you notice what your face looks like when you're listening to someone else speaking.

- **Check your volume**. Before you get on a video call, test your volume, if you can. Everyone at this point is getting a little annoyed when people ask, "Can you hear me now?" Also, try to connect through Bluetooth headphones if you have them.

- **Appear engaged.** It's important to look like you're engaged and actively listening. Don't forget that just because you aren't speaking doesn't mean you aren't being seen.

- **Invest in lighting**. If you're going to do virtual meetings routinely, or if you are interviewing for a job, make a small investment in appropriate lighting. You can tell when you're in a virtual meeting with people who are completely prepared. The setup behind them looks professional or interesting and there is balanced lighting on their face. This is extremely important for those with a darker complexion because the natural light in your home or office may not provide that balanced lighting that gives you a more positive appearance. Remember, there is a reason why Oscars are awarded to lighting technicians.

We have to acknowledge that many people are seeing themselves in a new light. Staring at that small image of yourself all through these virtual meetings can be a bit unnerving. Use this opportunity to be sure you are not overly critical of yourself. We can always find something we want to adjust. But instead, I challenge you to point out a positive characteristic about yourself the next time you think you see a flaw. You must fight negativity with positivity because life is about balance. And on the days you just need a break, if you are using Zoom, simply right-click the window that shows your face and click Hide Self View in your video settings.

Whether you like it or not, online and video technology is here to stay. Even if you only use them to have virtual happy hours with your friends or play games using apps such as Houseparty, video tools allow others to see you.

Sleeping Your Way to the Top Is So 1970s

I once had an employee who leaned forward, put her hands on her breasts, and said, "These are gonna get me places." She uttered those words at a company reception—toward the end of the party after a few hours of open bar—and her comment spread like wildfire. It followed her for the rest of her time at the organization. Drinking in a work setting is common at holiday parties, networking receptions, and so on, but you must be careful about how much alcohol you consume. You are always being watched, even when you think it's fine.

Many people have had an embarrassing scenario, where maybe they've had a few too many, but we must remember to be cautious. The unfortunate reality is we are always being judged based on what we say, wear, and, of course, what we do. Think of how close you are when you are speaking with another employee or customer. It is all being observed. I'm not saying it's right. I'm just saying it still happens. Apparently, reality TV just isn't enough for people. They want to create an entertaining story in their minds. When the time comes for you to grow in your company, any established storyline can be thrown into the discussion when leadership is reviewing your potential for advancement. It's hard enough for women to ascend to high-level positions. The last thing women need is something like this following them.

We will not waste precious pages going over what you should already know, but we will quickly say that maintaining your dignity is imperative to becoming a leader. In today's society, women are judged more harshly than men. According to a new analysis by the executive recruitment firm Korn Ferry, the average age of individuals holding C-suite titles (CEO, CHRO, CMO, CIO, CFO) is 56.[17] Be careful of decisions you make early in your career because it's a long journey ahead, and the numbers aren't in your favor.

Recognize Your Inner Strength

Executive presence isn't just physical, it's mental. At the end of the day, you still have to be yourself; but in leadership, you must be the most polished version of yourself.

People want to be inspired by those in leadership. We must constantly work to improve our presence and then mentor others. As we look at the business world from a global view, we observe that people in the workplace have a variety of speaking styles. One area I believe is not discussed enough and should be more often is that of constantly building our vocabulary and improving our professional presence. In the U.S., people may have a bias in the workplace against someone whose diction or speaking style differs from their own.

Summary

- Dress appropriately for your shape and age and be aware of current fashion trends.
- Style your hair professionally and be aware of the wide range of styles for various hair types.
- Invest in the appropriate equipment to maintain a professional image in the virtual world.
- Be your authentic self.
- Recognize your inner strength.

---

[17] Korn Ferry. "Age and Tenure in the C-Suite." https://www. kornferry.com/about-us/press/age-and-tenure-in-the-c-suite. Accessed August 22, 2021.

Accept Me for Who I Am

I grew up with a mother who was a feminist, former Black Panther, sociology professor, writer, trainer, and frequent guest on many of the popular talk shows during the 1990s and 2000s. Growing up, my mother moved us from Detroit, Michigan to Iowa so she could take an associate professor position at a distinguished college. One of my early memories was helping her create a new hairstyle on the back of her head. "These are called dreadlocks," she said, as I witnessed the birth of a new hairstyle she would wear for the next forty years. As I grew older, my mom told me she had wanted to wear a more natural hairstyle for a while, but she waited until she felt her position was secure before she felt like she could.

The irony of her decision regarding her personal hairstyle was that she was still allowing my grandmother to perm my hair. I remember my grandmother saying my curly hair was unmanageable and that it needed to be soft and straight. She was passing down the same beauty standard she had grown up with. It was a part of my routine, even after I got a really bad perm once that burned and damaged my scalp.

It was not until I went to college that a beautiful Black woman from Brooklyn convinced me my hair was nothing to be ashamed of. After my first year of college, I decided to grow my hair out, and it has been natural ever since. But the fairy tale does not end there. You see, I still felt it was necessary to straighten my hair before important dates, graduate school engagements, job interviews, and even for my wedding.

I would think about the implications of my image while resentfully flat-ironing my hair before an interview, with the intention of going back to my natural hair on the first day of work. This is what I felt I would have to do to attain steady employment. It was not until several years ago when I was interviewing for a promotion with the executive committee that the CFO walked in wearing a glorified, outstanding dreadlock mohawk. I was floored. I knew things had been changing in my industry but, frankly, I didn't realize how much. I got the job and remember telling her how much that experience impacted me. She said I should just be myself and never compromise, even for the important stuff.

A few years later, I took her advice for the biggest interview of my life: my first CEO position in association management. I remember driving to Baltimore for the interview with my husband on the phone, questioning if I had made the right decision about my hair. It was in full force: curly, fluffy, shiny, and beautiful. He, as others did before him, kept saying, "If they don't accept you for who you are, you don't want to work for them, anyway."

When I walked into that interview with 13 white women and men surrounding the board table and welcoming me to the third round of the interview process, I didn't feel insecure or scared the way I thought I would. In fact, I felt relieved and exuded confidence, no longer feeling like an imposter. I felt whole, empowered, and, most importantly, dignified. I nailed that interview and got the job.

When I was driving home, I called my mother and told her all about it. I then said, "Mom, I wore my hair completely natural." And she said, "Like you should." I realized then that while my mother had to wait to change her hair until she got her big break, I had the ability to be my true authentic self. I developed confidence and am grateful to those who saw me for my talent, knowledge, and presence. This time, things had changed for both of us.

—Dresden Farrand, MPA, MPP, CAE; CEO, American Water Resources Association

5

COMMUNICATION SKILLS ARE KEY

I magine preparing to go into battle. You ready your weapon, grit your teeth, and look toward the general at the top of the hill, who says, "Well, I don't know...maybe we should go this way, but I'm not sure. Want to check it out?"

Have you ever been in a meeting where a person in a position of power was doubting themselves out loud? Hearing such uncertainty is like nails on a chalkboard to me, especially in informative sessions when they are supposed to be leading a team in a certain direction. I recently attended a meeting during which a young professional was introduced as the acting director for her department due to the recent departure of their long-term leader. Even though she had many years' experience in that department, her body language and words gave the appearance that she was unsure of herself and lacked the confidence needed to fill the role long term. She sat with her shoulders slumped and kept her head down. When people turned to her with a question, she responded with her head down, as if it were her first day on the job. I had seen this acting director present the same information in previous meetings, but it was clear she was suddenly unsure of herself in this room full of executives. If I had known her better, I would have pulled her out of the room and given her a pep talk.

Be the General You'd Want to Follow

People desire a variety of strong attributes in a leader. One key attribute is confidence, not only in who you are as a person, but also in what you know. Women in the workplace must stop searching for validation in the room and take responsibility for believing in themselves first. The general should instill the troops with confidence, not vice versa. A strong leader can inspire and improve the odds of victory in the same way a weak leader can sabotage a good idea with weak words and actions. In other words, if *you* don't even believe in your idea, why would *they* bother to listen?

I am not saying a leader shouldn't gather buy-in or feedback, but when it's time to make a decision, make it. Be sure both your verbal and non-verbal communication show you believe in your decision and are confident. Below are a variety of exercises you can do to help you become more aware of your body language and vocal inflection.

Part 1: Body Language

Activity	Sit in front of a mirror as though you are in a meeting room.
Ask Yourself	What is my facial expression?
Think	Do I look sad or angry? Do I look unusually happy?
Examine	Are your shoulders slumped or are you slouching? Are your arms crossed? Do you look around the room as though you don't feel like you fit in or don't want to be there?

This exercise is a way to test common indicators of uncertainty. While practicing in front of the mirror may take some getting used to, it is an opportunity to examine your body language and make relevant changes that will improve your image as a leader.

The next time you walk into a meeting room,

- Sit up straight.
- Have an openness to your body that shows that you are willing to receive information.
- Look around the room and use positive eye contact to bring everyone into your conversation.

I have a co-worker who occasionally lets her frustration show through her body language. If she disagrees with the conversation in the room, she will slump down in her chair, rest her hands on her chin, and occasionally roll her eyes. Of course, we've all sat through a meeting where we felt as if leadership may not have been making the best decisions, but we can't allow our body language to show dissention.

Steeple Your Fingers

Steepling your fingers is when you place your hands together in the form of a triangle, fingertip to fingertip and thumb to thumb. This is also called the Triangle of Power. Whether you're standing and talking or sitting at a table, holding your hands in this position draws people in to listen to you as an authority figure. This power position is a key body language move that centers your posture. It says you are focused and that you know what you're talking about, but you are not threatening.

Part 2: Vocal

For many people, the number-one fear is public speaking, and the second is death. I often joke that people would rather be in the casket than give the eulogy. I recognize that not everyone is comfortable speaking in front of a group, but it's important to face your fears and strengthen your weaker spots in leadership. Presence isn't just your physical appearance, it's your mental attitude.

As we look at the business world through a global view, people in the workplace will have a variety of speaking styles. One thing that I think is not discussed, but should be, is constantly building our vocabulary and improving our professional presence. In the U.S., people may have a bias in the workplace against someone whose diction or speaking style is different from their own.

Early in my career when I was working in the D.C. area, I met a communications executive from South Carolina. He talked extensively about how difficult it was to be taken seriously in a communications or public relations firm in D.C. with his Southern drawl. I've had similar conversations with people from Massachusetts who said their coworkers would poke fun at them because of the way they pronounced certain words. Those same challenges can be true of people from different cultural backgrounds.

In my eyes, the following things need to happen simultaneously:

- From a personal perspective, as an American businesswoman, I always strive to expand and improve my vocabulary and work on my public speaking skills, whether it's through opportunities that are presented or by taking training through companies like ToastMasters™. It is always our responsibility to "dress for the job we want." When I say dress for the job we want, it's not just physically. However, we also must learn to confront our biases and listen to people through a different lens. We need to listen to the knowledge that people have and listen to the worlds they're saying, not just the accent they're saying it with.

- People should consider taking a writing course to become a better writer or take immersion classes if they want to learn a new language. What we often fail to practice is our presentation skills for growth in the business environment. How well do you articulate your message when pitching an idea to your boss?

- Avoid the use of lazy words. I will never forget, as a teenager, if I used the expression "you know" while telling my mother a story, she would respond by saying, "No, I don't know and that's why I'm listening to your story." She would put her hand on my shoulder, tell me to stop saying "you know," and asked me to tell her what I meant, specifically. So often, people don't recognize that the way they speak in a casual environment does not translate into the business environment.

- Practice avoiding filler words. When was the last time you turned on the news and heard them interviewing a CEO who used space fillers? Everyone has heard them at some point in their personal or professional career. These are the most common filler words to avoid:

  - Like
  - Sorry
  - Ah
  - You know
  - Um
  - I guess

These words may make you feel better as you search for what you really want to say, but I encourage you to avoid them. It is far more compelling to leave a pause in your conversation that allows an opportunity to draw people into what you are saying.

Trigger Phrases

Let's consider a few commonly used phrases in the workplace. As you read each phrase, take a moment to note the first thing that comes to mind.

Example #1: Can you do me a favor?

What is your first immediate thought when you hear someone ask, "Can you do me a favor?" Perhaps you are wondering what they really want. Maybe you are contemplating if you were the first person they approached, or if they have already asked other coworkers for the same favor.

When someone asks for a favor, a simple response such as "Sure, what's up?" implies you will help them, regardless of their request. The next time someone asks you this, try a different response, such as this:

"Well, it depends. What do you need?"

Time Management Tip:
Assess what your co-worker needs before you agree to anything.

If you're in a mid-level position and trying to showcase your leadership characteristics, it's important to assess what people need from you before making yourself available.

Let's think of another common workplace ask and contemplate how to respond.

Example #2: "Hey, do you have a second?"

This phrase can mean a variety of things, depending on who is asking. Most people have used this phrase at some point in their personal or professional lives. But as you ask people to respect *your* time in a leadership role, you also need to be mindful of *their* time. Will this request literally take only one second?

When someone asks you if you have a second, do you frequently answer "yes" or "sure" or "I think so"? Or are you honest about your time commitments? Many women have been socialized to say yes even when their plates are so full that responsibilities are falling off the edges. We must remember that leaders who inspire confidence are not afraid to say no. In fact, many leaders who say no are seen as busy and hardworking and are revered by their co-workers. These types of leaders have built a reputation that their time is valuable, so when someone asks them for a favor and they agree, their unexpected yes is often celebrated with public praise at a meeting with key stakeholders and decision makers.

Time Management Tip:
If it's not in writing, it doesn't exist.

Having too much on our plate is often the result of agreeing to tasks and assignments that take far longer than initially promised. Make sure you get a detailed written summary of expectations to ensure you truly understand the task at hand before agreeing to help. In the future, ask, "Can you please email me what you're looking for so I can assess what's needed?"

We often fall into the habit of being the go-to person, and people get accustomed to us saying yes. When this happens, we can be afraid of how we would come across if we said no. Sadly, the public praise and thank-you lunches often go to the person who helped with only one or two major projects instead of the person who played an integral role in five, even though both had stepped outside of their direct job responsibilities.

Symbolism in Communication

Symbolism in communication includes paying attention to how we treat women as compared to men and to differences between races. It also encompasses being more aware of today's over-hyped environment, the need for balance, and to recognize simple misunderstandings.

I think blogger Catherine Leclair, who wrote the article, "I'm A Woman, Shake My Hand Damn It" made a great point: "I'm actually offended when I'm out with my husband and I'll see a man give him a firm handshake...then, I get this dainty little finger shake."[18]

The flimsy handshake symbolizes a pervasive thought process which operates under the guise of respect. In reality, what if this deliberate intention to avoid mistreating others sometimes has the opposite effect? A handshake is the symbol of agreement and respect. In business, it's almost like an unwritten contract. When your handshake is firm, it means you stand by your word and can be trusted. While no one wants the full-force, bone-crushing handshake assault, in a professional setting, it's important to be consistent and give people a proper handshake, regardless of their gender.

The consistent and pervasive headlines about sexism from the #MeToo movement remind me of the early 2010s when it seemed as though nearly every headline was accusing someone of yet another form of mistreatment: racism. These headlines were emanating from everyday schoolteachers to celebrities to politicians. A large number of these accusations were justified, but as the headlines about racism continued, it seemed to have a hidden impact that few truly realized. Over time, many people who felt they treated others equally became more and more frustrated

---

[18] LeClair, Catherine. "I'm A Woman, Shake My Hand, Damn It." *Deadspin*, August 3, 2017. https://deadspin.com/i-m-a-woman-shake-my-hand-damn-it-1796885540. Accessed August 22, 2021.

by the daily headlines and accusations of racism. For many, it seemed as though no matter what they said or did, they would inevitably face the prospect of being called a racist in a comments section or in person, simply for being who they were. When people feel they have no voice or as if they are being pre-judged, they often tune out or stopped caring.

When I use the word *care*, I am not saying people fail to care about others, but rather that ignoring the debate became a sort of coping mechanism for some. As people grew tired of the anger and division on social media, in blogs, and in person, it seemed many had a similar take away: this entire thing is exhausting.

Think: Can Hypersensitivity Stifle Your Growth?

Ask yourself two honest questions:

- How sensitive are you?
- What are your professional goals?

If your goal is never to encounter a single person who says something offensive, you can absolutely accomplish it by locking your doors and never venturing outside. There is a difference between a deliberate hateful comment and an off-color remark that lies in a gray area. If these types of remarks are ingrained into the culture at your workplace, I would recommend you seek a job at a more inclusive workplace. But if you encounter these comments sporadically in your everyday interactions with people, you have to assess how you want to respond. The strange truth is, when people feel comfortable around you, from time to time, they may not watch their tone and say things that might not be politically correct in some circumstances. With trust, you can find teachable moments. But remember that with the judgment of others comes loss of trust. No one should ever tolerate overtly hateful or insulting remarks. But if you find yourself in that gray area, please consider whether your reaction to these types of comments is worth stifling your growth.

The 3 Cs

As you move forward in improving your communication, remember these three Cs for success in any business or personal relationship:

- Communication
- Coordination
- Compromise

Now, some of you might be thinking, "Don't you mean collaboration instead of coordination?" Well, collaboration is important within one team or department when discussing ideas and courses of action, but coordination is important when two or more departments or teams are working together. When new ideas and courses of action are being taken, there must be a synergy of effort and alignment with the overall company vision, mission, and strategy. In a fast-paced world in which we are responding to emails at a rapid pace and making decisions that lack face-to-face communication, it is imperative we recognize the importance of coordination. In addition, the ability to seek common ground and compromise is an important tool for any successful leader. Give and take are often required to find alignment and move your initiatives forward.

Like the old saying says, "Life is ten percent what happens to you and ninety percent how you react to it."

Summary

- Be confident.
- Be aware of your body language.
- Practice public speaking and avoid filler words.
- Notice trigger phrases and how requests affect your time management.
- Pay attention to symbolism in communication.
- Remember the 3 Cs: Communicate, Coordinate, and Compromise.

Tips from an Executive Recruiter

Through my work as an executive recruiter, I have had the opportunity to observe hundreds of candidates interview with clients for leadership roles, negotiate for themselves, and have also had to do a fair bit of negotiation myself! Too often, I see female candidates diminishing their accomplishments, being passed over for opportunities, crediting others for their work, and failing to self-inform and self-advocate in compensation conversations. Regardless of whether we *should* have to focus on how we present and package ourselves to others, it's critical to consider the importance of the impression we make, what people take away from non-verbal cues, and how to best convey information authoritatively.

I've had the chance to witness some amazing leaders who command a room, relate well with others, and have an art for delivering an unpopular message while also displaying sensitivity, empathy, and compassion. A few tips I have learned along the way include:

- **Sing your own praises, no one else will do it for you.** While it's important to credit the team for their contributions, there are times when it is appropriate to own your personal wins! Keep track of the things you have been responsible for development, new programs you have created, deals you have sold.

- **Sit in the front of the room**. I often see women come into Board meetings and take a seat at the far end of the table or the back of the room. Don't do that! Everyone in the room has earned their seat at the table. Get into the center of the action, be a part of the conversation, and share your expertise.

- **Be a "Superperson."** When I am speaking publicly, engaging in a tough conversation over the phone, or negotiating for myself or someone else, I always prefer to do so while standing, ideally in the Superman pose. Something about standing up straight, letting the air move through my body, and speaking with conviction makes me feel powerful. Give it a try!

- **Practice makes perfect**. We've all heard it many times, but it is hard to argue the effectiveness of knowing your material, feeling confident in what you are presenting, and anticipating what some of the challenges to what you have to say might be. You may not need to envision the audience in their birthday suits; but getting into their heads and thinking about how they may react to the news you are delivering, the proposal you have shared, or the risks associated with taking a certain path will be enormously helpful in confidently responding to others.

—Stephanie Tomasso, Managing Director and Global Association Practice Leader, Russell Reynolds Associates

6

LEADING IN A TIME OF CRISIS

A famous quote states that one should never let a good crisis go to waste. It is human nature to get caught up in everyday routines and avoid making changes to a business operation in times of relative stability. So often, companies wait until their organization or the environment is in crisis before they review their operation and respond. Credit Suisse has found that the average lifespan of a company listed on the S&P 500 fell from almost 60 years in the 1950s to less than 20 years today.[19] Technology and disruption have changed how modern businesses operate. The more prepared any company is to not only react to a changing environment but adjust before a crisis will determine its longevity. A strong leader should look at the company's potential—not just the current processes, products, and services.

[19] Sheetz, Michael. "Technology Killing off Corporate America: Average Life Span of Companies under 20 Years." *CNBC*, August 24, 2017. https://www.cnbc.com/2017/08/24/technology-killing-off-corporations-average-lifespan-of-company-under-20-years.html. Accessed August 22, 2021.

In late 2019, my company created a new program. The first Women Executives in Building Summit was developed to highlight, celebrate, and provide networking opportunities for C-suite women who work in the building industry. The purpose of the first event was to bring together women in the C-suite from building related associations. In my opinion, it starts with that group recognizing its role in this space for the predominately male members of the industry to recognize their own strengths. In addition, it would be more effective for each of us to seek women in the C-suite within our own respective industries and bring them all together for the next year's event.

At the 2019 event, I moderated a panel of two female leaders in the built environment association space and Dawn Sweeney, then-CEO of the National Restaurant Association. Dawn is highly respected and was chosen by the industry magazine *CEO Update* as their 2018 CEO of the Year. The executives in the audience asked Dawn how she managed so much at one time and she shared a phrase that resonated with the attendees and almost became the unofficial mantra of the meeting.

"At work, you have glass and rubber balls," Dawn said. "And you also have glass and rubber balls in your personal life. If it's a rubber ball, you can let it drop, bounce, and get it on the way back. But if a glass ball drops, it shatters." Dawn stared out into the audience and challenged the room of female executives to recognize what kind of balls they were juggling.

Glass Balls, Rubber Balls

Deciding what responsibilities should be put on the back burner is an essential skill in business. However, it's more than just your schedule. You often have to find a way to communicate with your team to let them know how to adjust. While you never want to drop a ball, sometimes things come up and you have to decide where to focus your time and energy. Whether in the workplace or in your everyday life, sometimes you have to say no to get someone to value your yes.

That message was so important to share, and there were so many more great messages of strategy and progress from this amazing panel of leaders. The women in the room also took time to network with each other and share their own personal stories. Everyone agreed this was an important dialogue, and most have continued it to this day. In 2020, we turned the event into a quarterly virtual leadership series. As you can imagine, 2020 brought additional industry challenges, and it was important for these women to have discussions and share with each other.

I would like to shine a light on Mary Barra, CEO of General Motors. She was elected Chair of the GM Board of Directors on January 4, 2016, and has served as CEO since January 15, 2014. After the homicide of George Floyd in Minneapolis and the protests that followed across the country and around the world, many corporate leaders made statements. Mary Barra had already begun to improve diversity and inclusion within the board of General Motors, including making it the first automobile board of directors with 55 percent women and the first Fortune 500 company to achieve parity. However, according to their 2019 sustainability report, she also sets a bold aspiration—to be the most inclusive company in the world.[20] Barra stated, "Let's stop asking 'why' and start asking 'what.' What are we going to do?"

In addition, GM's sustainability report confirmed that, in 2020, Barra commissioned and chaired an Inclusion

---

[20] "2019 Sustainability Report 2019, 3." General Motors. Available for download at https://www.gmsustainability.com/downloads-and-archives.html. Accessed August 22, 2021.

Advisory Board of both internal and external leaders. I was impressed by her words: "Awareness leads to dialogue... dialogue leads to understanding...and understanding leads to change. It has never been clearer that what we at GM are doing to advance equity and inclusion is not enough."

So rarely do leaders admit that what they have done is not enough. In order for companies to improve and transform in a time of crisis, they must admit the realities they are facing, listen to their employees and customers, and then take an intentional approach to change.

There are many examples of change that can come from leadership in a time of crisis—specifically, looking through the lens of change as an opportunity for growth and not a temporary holding pattern to get back to the way things used to be. I've heard many leaders talk about how they can't wait to get back to "normal" instead of looking at the new virtual tools and programs that were developed from this pandemic and reviewing how they can adopt new policy for the changing environment. We must learn from every crisis and use it as a springboard to make adjustments that you should have prepared for years ago.

Again, as I mentioned, women leaders often have a different style for leading in a crisis. During the COVID-19 pandemic, countries led by women had better results and a lower death count. New Zealand's Prime Minister Jacinda Kate Laurell Ardern exhibited tremendous leadership skills while the world battled the COVID-19 pandemic. In February 2020, before New Zealand had any recorded cases, Ardern banned any foreigners coming from or through China from entering the country. Ardern put lockdowns in place quickly and successfully contained the coronavirus when the U.S. struggled and had increasing numbers.

Several news articles stated that she took the necessary steps and made no apologies for closing the borders and imposing quarantines.[21] In New Zealand, masks, lockdowns, and social distancing all but ended in October 2020 because of her crisis management skills. New Zealand had a total of 26 deaths and an average of 320 cases per million, whereas the United States had 25,000 cases per million. Those same articles noted that her handling of the pandemic fueled her recent election victory.

Think Outside the Box

When the COVID-19 pandemic arrived, we were reminded of the importance of looking at our business differently—specifically, focusing on identifying new challenges our members and the industry as a whole would now be facing and adapting programs and services accordingly. But as business leaders, we should always focus on adaptability and preparedness. How many executives at Kodak should have embraced the digital future before Shutterfly dominated their business? In the end, the only way to stay in the game was to buy their competitor. How many convention and visitors' bureaus should have established a quality digital tour of their city prior to the pandemic?

Creativity to Compete

A virtual world puts a pause on fancy dinners, fun events, and one-on-one, in-person networking with your peers. For those who participate as volunteer leaders who share their ideas and guide the strategic direction of an organization,

---

[21] Smith, Alexander. "New Zealand's Jacinda Ardern wins big after world-leading Covid-19 response." *NBC Universal News Group*, October 20, 2020. https://www.nbcnews.com/news/world/new-zealand-s-jacinda-ardern-wins-big-after-world-leading-n1243972. Accessed August 22, 2021.

things have changed. When the meeting is over, we click End Meeting. No networking, no goodbye handshake, no cheers or toasts to the strategic guidance—it all seems very impersonal and unsustainable without thinking creatively.

One thing I incorporated into my board meetings is more time for discussion. I surprise our board members with a food or beverage delivery the day before the meeting. As highly sought-after experts in their fields, it's not that our volunteer leaders can't pay for their own dinner. But as my mom taught me long ago, it's the thought that counts. Little touches and notes of thanks. Sweet treats or connecting something personal you know about your leaders will help show you care and value their input. I believe utilizing a little creativity makes a difference in a virtual environment.

Inspire Your Team

Sometimes it's easier said than done, but we need to do more than tell our teams we appreciate them. We must also show them. In a time of crisis, everyone is dealing with different burdens at home and at work. Although managers are not psychologists, sometimes it just takes small connections or actions to show your team you're listening, that you care, and that you value their work.

Rethink Team Building

When the COVID-19 pandemic forced my company, the National Institute of Building Sciences, to work remotely, I made a point of keeping our team meetings fun. One of our favorite weekly activities was called "NIBS Cribs"—a play on the popular early 2000s *MTV* show *MTV Cribs*, which took viewers through a celebrity's home. Each week, we had a tour of a different employee's home. Each staff member went above and beyond to make it enjoyable by including fun soundtracks and having their kids or spouse serve as hosts. One of my favorite moments was when our team member Sarah stood at her front door and said, "As you'll see, the fountains are turned off today and the Maserati is in the shop, so we're using the Ford Explorer." It made me realize that for so many of us, work is like a second home. Even when you cannot bring the team together, finding memorable activities to create shared experiences is essential. Not everyone on the team volunteered to show off their home, and there was no pressure to do so. It was important for people to feel comfortable sharing and remembering that this was just to have some fun and break away from the everyday work.

We utilized The Very Interesting Game to engage my team and create team-building in a new and unique way. This card game was invented by Deedre Daniel, the founder of The Interesting Conversations Company whose mission is to help people think more creatively, laugh, and build stronger bonds with others.

Since I mentioned Deedre, I want to take a moment to pause the conversation about team-building and share a little more about fearless leadership. Let me tell you a little bit about the owner of this company. Deedre had a stellar 19-year corporate career at GEICO, where she rapidly rose through the ranks from a front-line sales associate to the head of the Affinity Marketing Department, where she managed a $50 million marketing budget and strategy for over 800 partner organizations. Although, for multiple years, her division was rated as outstanding in annual performance evaluations and was often touted as the company's secret weapon, she felt her career beginning to stall and promotional opportunities fading around her. In 2018, she left all that security behind for an elevated title and more lucrative pay at another company—only to be let go at the end of the year. In 2019, she plunged her life savings into starting The Interesting Conversations Company and a nonprofit called The Big Fat Tip, which collects donations to provide surprise $1,000 tips to workers in the U.S. service industry.

At the beginning of 2020, her business started to take off. People were calling her daily to book speaking and corporate training events long into the future. Then COVID-19 arrived and ended all in-person events around the world. Her entire business model was based on in-person events, and all of her future jobs and opportunities instantly disappeared. Due to the timing of her launch, she didn't qualify for most of the federal programs, grants, and safety nets. Her husband's second job with the XFL, which he had taken on to help make ends meet, also instantly vanished when the XFL declared bankruptcy. Since it was a part-time job, he did not qualify for benefits there, either. But she did not let that hold her back. Despite being afraid and not knowing where the money would come from, Deedre immediately adapted and turned her business into a virtual team-building and engagement game.

She was already a powerhouse speaker and when she developed the game, she channeled all of that energy into a truly exciting virtual event that was perfect for both business and personal events. This story is key to the topic of leading in a time of crisis because she did not pause to feel sorry for herself, talk about how she couldn't travel, or worry that quitting her job might have been the wrong decision. No, instead she looked for the new opportunity. She looked at the changing environment and the personal isolation and turned her business into a type of self-help clinic for those feeling trapped in their homes. It was a personal release, a new way to learn about your co-workers and friends. Plus, she keeps it fresh, adding new decks, writing unique cards for corporate sponsors, creating new stories, and designing some pretty entertaining wardrobes if you choose to have a theme.

Deedre found a way to adapt her business to a virtual environment and engage companies from around the world, helping bring new conversations to light and truly build a team environment. I think everyone can learn a lesson from what she brings to the table. She always looks to advance herself and her career, and to give back to others while continuing to move forward.

Take a Trip to Paris

I have found it's important to engage other members of the team when selecting these team-building experiences. My next team-building event was selected by a few members of the staff. They found tour guides in Paris had begun giving virtual tours, as tourists were no longer walking around in the city. It was wonderful to open the next weekly staff meeting with the statement, "I'm taking the team to Paris... virtually." After getting over the disappointment that we were not all flying to Paris (clearly, since the EU was still closed to U.S. visitors), the team was happy to hear the virtual tour included an actual French cheese and wine tasting.

Summary

- Take advantage of a crisis to make process and program improvements.
- Be aware of what you are juggling and don't drop any glass balls.
- Listen and take an intentional approach to change.
- Think outside the box to innovate programs and services in your company.
- Rethink team building by testing out non-traditional activities and ask for feedback from your staff for ideas.

Aspire to Be a True Team Player

As a middle-school student, I was far from athletic. But I went to a school where everyone was encouraged to get involved in some type of intramural sport, and so I chose basketball. We had a great coach who encouraged spirit over talent, so I felt valued and included even though I was not much of a scorer!

We were a competitive team and pretty successful in our league—one year, making it all the way to the regional finals. There was, of course, a great deal of excitement about this, and we were very dedicated to winning. And although we won, I have long considered our game a failure, and one of my greatest life lessons.

The score, as we entered the final quarter, was close. I had the ball and was making my way to the other end of the court when another player (indeed, one of my own teammates) tripped me—clearly on purpose. She grabbed the dropped ball, drove down the court, and scored. I was stunned. And upset.

To be sabotaged by someone on the opposing team is one thing (still not good), but to be taken down by one of your own—that was something I had never considered. From that moment on, I dedicated myself to being a team player in all that I did. And team players get rewarded in ways that are incalculable and enduring.

—Dawn Sweeney, President & CEO Emerita, National Restaurant Association

7

DRINKS WITH THE BOYS

In March 2017, bloggers and media reacted to former Vice President Mike Pence's comments from 2002 when he told *The Hill* he never eats alone with a woman other than his wife and that he won't attend events featuring alcohol without her by his side, either.[22] This was a few months before the #MeToo movement went viral and, at the time, a large number of people felt his comment was insensitive and sexist because he was essentially grouping all women together. While men could have access to dinners, even world leaders like German chancellor Angela Merkel, a major ally which boasts the world's fourth largest economy, would potentially be shut out of the high-level conversations with Pence.

---

[22] Parker, Ashley. "Karen Pence Is the Vice President's 'Prayer Warrior,' Gut Check and Shield." *The Washington Post*, March 28, 2017. https://www.washingtonpost.com/politics/karen-pence-is-the-vice-presidents-prayer-warrior-gut-check-and-shield/2017/03/28/3d7a26ce-0a01-11e7-8884-96e6a6713f4b_story.html?tid=a_inl&utm_term=.b44444e74bd6. Accessed August 22, 2021.

Others celebrated Pence's admission as being respectful to his wife, but I wonder how these comments would be perceived in our current social climate where men are increasingly being held accountable for harassment and accusations of improper behavior. I am finding more and more of my male friends feel they are walking on eggshells, and that any interaction with the wrong woman could lead to life-changing ramifications, both socially and professionally.

As men across the country are starting to acknowledge how just one negative interaction with a member of the opposite sex can impact a person's career, we have to recognize this isn't exactly a brand-new concept. Women have been waking up with anxiety about being harassed by a coworker and leaving jobs they loved because they felt they had no other choice. They may hold their keys between their fingers as they walk down a dark street, looking over their shoulder as they open their door, and live in their own fear of one bad interaction with the wrong man.

While many men are recognizing the impact of one negative encounter with the wrong woman, for women throughout history, having one negative encounter with a man has not been the exception: it has been the rule. Let's use this new understanding to shape a world in which we all operate with a shared mutual respect. To do this, we need to have an honest conversation about this era of accusations and make sure we do not use it as an excuse to shut women out of the room under the guise of being respectful.

An article by Erin Duffy of *Fortune* says, "Socializing outside of the office is a large part of business, and if women aren't able to attend unless accompanied by a chaperone, then we're at a major disadvantage."[23] In a world where

---

[23] Duffy, Erin. "How Mike Pence's Dumb Dinner Rule Puts Women at a Disadvantage." *Fortune*, April 5, 2017. https://fortune.com/2017/04/05/mike-pence-wife-dinner/. Accessed August 22, 2021.

many promotions are based on conversations that occur outside of traditional business hours, giving men this exclusive social access presents an unfair advantage based on gender. Many might say women should respond by only having drinks with the girls, but having a mandate for divided social interactions would be a detriment to most organizations.

I will never forget, at one of my first jobs, a situation a young woman should never be caught up in. I was a few weeks into the job and we had a board meeting out of town. I was so excited to go on a business trip and didn't know about all the baggage that comes with work travel. It was toward the end of a long day of meetings when two other female staff members and I went to the bar. Now, I didn't drink in college nor at the start of my career, but as a new employee I was excited to be invited to get to know these two ladies better.

This was my first association job. Associations are mission-driven nonprofit organizations that serve the professions or industries they represent. When we walked over to the bar, a few of the board members were already there, and it looked like they had been there a while. We were not there long, but before I knew it, one of the girls was being asked to let a member take a body shot off of her neck. I was new, so no one was bothering me, but I will never forget the look on her face. This look of confusion, shame, and fear. Do you say no to the member and risk getting fired? Do you say yes and risk getting fired? Before I knew it, she had said yes. And when we got back to the office, she was fired. It was an early life lesson for me about women and men in the workplace and who pays the price for bad behavior.

The women who work in the association industry have so many of these stories to share. Not too long ago, I was speaking with an executive in the hospitality industry. I told her about my start in the association world and she shared a few stories about working in the hotel industry. As a female executive, Rhonda had a lot of challenging experiences. She shared several life lessons and plenty of food for thought for women who enter a male-dominated industry.

She talked about tips she had learned over the years for women who can do well and avoid finding themselves in awkward or uncomfortable situations. We both discussed how these jobs often required knowing how to manage alcohol. So many work events have a reception, or happy hour, or simply a dinner with clients. She talked about how clients expect others in the hospitality industry to drink along with them. They want not only to break bread with you, but often to share a bottle of wine or other alcoholic beverages.

Have you ever attended a reception with members or customers and been asked, "Where is your drink?" If you don't want to drink, do you often feel pressured to have one anyway? We do hope people will allow individuals to make their own decisions about whether to drink at work events. But it is often a topic of conversation, especially when people are applying for jobs in these highly social positions. Rhonda and I discussed the following tips for drinking at work functions:

- **Soda water with lime**.
  If you don't want to drink and also don't want to explain your decision to others, you can order a soda water and lime from the bar. Request a short glass. Having that beverage often allows you to continue to socialize with customers without answering the question, "Where is your drink?" It can also help avoid those people who feel uncomfortable drinking in front of someone who is not drinking.
- **Pace yourself**.
  When socializing at work functions that include alcohol, it is important to pace yourself. There is no reason to drink too quickly and risk becoming

intoxicated. I've seen people cross that line and start stumbling on their words at the table with customers—or worse, stumbling across the room. The shocked faces and negative body language from customers is not something you want to encounter in your professional career.

- **Always remember to hydrate**. Water is your friend.

- **Be yourself; don't be pressured**.

  If you're not a drinker, then don't drink. Everyone should be able to be themselves in the work environment. No one should feel pressured to drink if they do not want to. I have a non-drinking friend who has had a very successful career in the hospitality industry. Everyone knows she does not drink, but that does not hold her back. She is fun to be around and makes her clients feel special, and that is what matters. She is also a foodie, so she makes the dining experience special. She keeps her clients happy by letting them order whatever they want, so they are not paying attention to the fact that she is not drinking.

- **Know when to leave.**

- Women can often find themselves in uncomfortable situations if they stay at the bar too long with a primarily male group. You hear the story time and time again: everything was fine until someone had one drink too many and made a pass or behaved in some other inappropriate way. We recognize men should be able to control themselves, and it shouldn't be a woman's responsibility to leave. However, I've always had a rule of leaving every party while the party is still fun. Don't wait until the bitter end. No good can come from it.

Many years ago, I was at a work event and went out with a group of co-workers to grab a drink at a bar near our hotel. We all shared how we thought the event went that day and got caught up on what was happening in each other's lives. It started to get a little late, so I wanted to head back to the hotel. There were five of us altogether. Four of us wanted to go back, but one guy wanted to stay. My employee said she would stay with him for one more drink. I had heard stories about this guy, so I tried to encourage her to come back with the rest of us, reminding her we had an early start the next day. But she didn't get the hint and said, "I'll be fine." The next day, she called me and we met somewhere private to talk. She was in tears. She said he made a pass and tried to touch her. She immediately left but was really stunned and hurt because she didn't think there should have been any issue–after all, he was married. She couldn't believe a married man would do that and felt embarrassed. It was not her fault. She was playing the role of the good co-worker and didn't want him to have to sit there by himself. She had thought they could spend the time getting to know each other better. Sometimes, in circumstances like this, it is better to play it safe and not to place yourself in situations where alcohol can unexpectedly change someone's behavior.

Back to my friend Rhonda. She told me another story about when she was a new general manager at a major hotel brand. She had attended a meeting with almost 100 other general managers from across the country, and women made up less than 10 percent of the group. She said she noticed a little later into the night that people had started disappearing. She asked where everyone was going and one of the guys said, "The strip club! Come with us." She paused and decided that if she was going to fit in and learn to connect with the rest of the team, then she had better join them. I asked her if she regrets going now, and she immediately answered no. She said it wasn't as bad as she thought it would be. She had been able to listen to twenty-year industry veterans discuss key customers and how to win them over and learn the strategies they used to grow their business. In addition, the guys were so happy she had hung out with the team that she earned a lot of street cred with the other general managers.

Lastly, Rhonda also noticed many of the men were sitting around talking about the stock market. She said her circle of women never talked about stocks. This may be something I'm just not aware of, but it seems men talk about stocks more than women do in their social circles. And we all know wealth is driven by engagement in the stock market and making wise financial decisions for yourself. Rhonda noted she had never realized how much the men in her office talked about stock tips, yet in her social circle of female groups, the topic never came up. She learned from her male counterparts about the importance of investing in the stock market, doing your research, and staying aware of the trends.

It's clear there is still a lot of work to do as it relates to minority women in the stock market. In 2017, Lauren Simmons became the first African American women to trade stocks full time on the floor of the U.S. Stock Exchange in their 228 year history.[24] She now spends a great deal of time educating women about the importance of investing in stocks.

Now, there may be plenty of women across the country who talk about investing. But for those who don't, this is a reminder that it's important not only to take steps to attain leadership but also to know what to do with the money earned when goals are achieved.

Many years later, at another company, I passed by my boss's office one afternoon and he asked if I was available to talk. I immediately began to think about our month-in

---

[24] Connley, Courtney. "The NYSE's Youngest Female Trader on Diversity in Finance: Employers Need 'to Stop Making Plans and Just Do It.'" *CNBC*. January 12, 2021. https://www.cnbc.com/2020/06/24/nyse-youngest-female-trader-lauren-simmons-on-diversity-in-finance.html. Accessed August 22, 2021.

sales numbers and whether I had sent my quarterly update. He said he had noticed I always seemed to have the right answers in meetings, but it bothered the others at the table. He closed by saying, "Try not to be so right all the time." The rest of our conversation went as follows:

"Am I dominating the conversation in the group discussion?" I asked. His answer was no.

"Am I talking over others when they're speaking?"

"No, it's not that," he answered. "People just don't like that you always seem to have the right answers."

Now, I have to wonder: would he have the same conversation with a man?

The onus is on all of us to have a more inclusive culture because the results have shown women in leadership more than hold their own. Market analytics firm MSCI released the "Women on Boards" study which states, "Companies in the MSCI World Index with strong female leadership generated a Return on Equity of 10.1% per year versus 7.4% for those without."[25] According to *Business Insider*, companies with women in leadership roles "crush the competition."[26] And The Peterson Institute for International Economics released a 2016 study that reports a positive correlation between the presence of women in corporate leadership and performance "in a magnitude that is not small."[27]

---

[25] Lee, Linda-Eling. "The Tipping Point: Women on Boards and Financial Performance." *MSCI*, December 16, 2016. https://www.msci.com/www/blog-posts/the-tipping-point-women-on/0538249725. Accessed August 22, 2021.

[26] Archer, Seth.. "Companies with Women in Leadership Roles Crush the Competition." *Business Insider*, June 17, 2016. https://www.businessinsider.com/companies-with-women-in-leadership-roles-perform-better-2016-6. Accessed August 22, 2021.

[27] Noland, Marcus, Tyler Moran, and Barbara Kotschwar. 2016. "Is Gender Diversity Profitable? Evidence from a Global Survey." *Peterson Institute for International Economics*, February 2016. https://www.piie.com/publications/working-papers/gender-

We have to think beyond the mindset of *us* versus *them* because the data shows a leadership team that features men and women working together significantly benefits the bottom line. Having some level of diversity translates into a more financially stable company that can put more money in people's paychecks. We need to keep an open dialogue and work together to address this issue. There isn't a pat answer for all circumstances.

"I raise up my voice—not so I can shout, but so that those without a voice can be heard...we cannot succeed when half of us are held back."
—Malala Yousafzai

I don't want the next generation to grow up and face the prospect of being shut out of leadership retreats and off-site strategy meetings because of the fear of accusations. Just as couples in successful relationships work as a team, we must all work as a team to create a world we aspire to live in–a world in which people from all walks of life feel the freedom and safety to achieve their dreams.

The overwhelming majority of companies have predominantly male leadership, which means the next generation of board members and leaders in the C-suite and executives must learn to interact with employees, regardless of gender. This is why we need unity, cohesion, and the flow of great ideas that come as a benefit of having the entire team included. We should strive to have leadership that is representative of the country in which we all live.

---

diversity-profitable-evidence-global-survey. Accessed August 22, 2021.

If Men Are from Mars and Women Are from Venus, Can We Find Common Ground on Earth?

In this current social climate, I am hearing more and more of my male friends saying they feel men are being given an automatic zero when they interact with women. I've had many conversations with professional contacts in my network who have confided in me, and they all shared a similar message:

"I feel like no matter what I would say or do, someone might accuse me of harassment."

First and foremost, we have to understand and empathize with the pain of harassment. We must use this unique moment in history to support the basic expectations of equality and safety across the board. Today, it seems as though we're being torn further and further apart. Many of the conversations I've had made me think of so many who are fearful of saying or doing the wrong thing around women, and that leads us to the sad cause and effect so many of us face.

If	A man is nervous about saying the wrong thing around women.
And	A woman over-scrutinizes every statement being made.
Then	The woman may find herself being excluded from important meetings or business trips.

While seeing it laid out like this may lead to a collective shrug, we need to have balance and recognize the difference between comments that are slightly inappropriate and the bold, blatant statements that cross the line and are just plain wrong. Women may find themselves being excluded because men just don't feel like being on their best behavior. And a male co-worker may feel so nervous that he chooses to leave women out of the conversation altogether. When I say "best behavior," I don't mean not getting wasted at a bar or going to a strip club. I simply mean the feeling that comes from not having every word out of your mouth over-scrutinized. We must find balance and respect for each other.

Summary

- Operate with shared mutual respect.
- Pace yourself and hydrate in work settings that include alcohol.
- Be yourself and don't feel pressured to drink or participate in activities that make you uncomfortable.
- Know when to leave a party.
- Build a leadership team that is representative of the diverse makeup of your country.

Stand Up to Stand Out

I entered the association management profession as the second professional woman in an association with a staff of 250 employees. Women were prevalent in the organization, but as assistants and secretaries, not as salaried managers. On my third day of work, I was invited to attend the company golf outing. On my sixth day of work, I was uninvited. It was an all-male event and the person who invited me mistakenly thought I could join. The outing was to take place in a couple of weeks, and I learned the men did not even have to take personal time off because it was a company-sponsored event. I made my disappointment and sense of unfairness known to my boss and colleagues, but since I was very new to the organization, I focused on being a better manager than any of the men there.

A few weeks later, we had an all-staff meeting. At the conclusion of the meeting, the CEO (whom I had not met) sought me out. He told me he had heard I was unhappy about the all-male golf outing and asked me what the problem was! This is how I explained it to him: "If you have an open position and two, equally qualified people apply for the job, which one would you be most likely to promote? The one you know because you spent time together at a golf outing or the one you don't know very well?" He looked at me, nodded his head, and said, "The one I know better–I see your point."

The next year, the men all had to take personal time off to attend the golf outing. And the year after, it was open to all salaried employees. A small victory for sure, but it taught me the importance of having the courage and tenacity to voice my opinion. I have never stopped doing that.

—Pat Blake, CEO, Heart Rhythm Society

8

UNCONSCIOUS BIAS

It starts so young. I believe people take for granted how early bias is taught to young boys and girls. It is almost like death and taxes. It is a guarantee that people all over the world cannot help but exhibit some type of unconscious bias toward one another. It is rarely on purpose, thus the term *unconscious*, yet it plagues society as a whole and many of the decisions we make as individuals.

It could be as simple as telling a young boy he is strong and telling a young girl she's pretty. It is the clothing manufacturers that label young boys' clothes with words like Adventurer, Doctor, or Hero while labeling young girls' clothes with words like Pretty and images of the sun, cats, or unicorns. It is setting up classes or activities for child-rearing with names like Mommy and Me, which automatically exclude fathers from child development activities. It's labeling men as leaders and women as caretakers.

Listen to the words you say to young kids and pay attention to the stereotypes that are used. Watch how boys and girls and men and women are portrayed on television and in YouTube videos. What is the gender balance between leadership roles?

And, of course, addressing racial bias presents yet another level of challenges. Sometimes it can be as simple as not having a diverse friend group, professional circle, or diversity in your general environment. That may not seem like a big deal to you. Why does it matter if your professional or social circles have diversity at all levels? I hope to answer that question in this chapter.

It is often said people fear what they don't understand. If we, as a society, do not make intentional efforts to broaden our circle of influence and our knowledge of other communities and recognize our differences, we will always see challenges in accepting those who are not like us. I pose the following questions to parents, grandparents, uncles, and aunts:

- No matter what community you grew up in, what do you do to expose young children in your family to people who look different from you?
- How do they learn? What do they see? And what do they hear from you?

The numbers don't lie and all the data shows that the more diverse an organization, the more financially successful it will be.[28] However, in my opinion, people by nature seek to socialize and work with whom they have commonalities. That may mean you look for someone who went to the same college. Or you may look for someone who looks and sounds like you and will, therefore, fit into the company culture better. I challenge everyone to assess their company culture and have a better understanding of the positive or negative culture that has been created due to lack of diversity in your leadership roles.

---

[28] Dixon-Fyle, Sundiatu, Kevin Dolan, Vivian Hunt, and Sara Prince. "Diversity wins: How inclusion matters." *McKinsey & Company*, May 19, 2020. https://www.mckinsey.com/featured-insights/diversity-and-inclusion/diversity-wins-how-inclusion-matters. Accessed August 22, 2021.

Companies are beginning to invest in training to address unconscious bias and trying to even out the opportunities. However, any substantive, long-term change will require people to recognize the bias that's taught when we are young and to make intentional changes. There are a variety of biases we could discuss, but I will focus on the challenges faced due to gender and racial bias.

Like gender bias, racial bias starts young and follows us through our adult life. One example is the research that shows the history of discrimination in the home appraisal market. Data from the Brookings Institution explains this history and shows Black-owned properties are undervalued by 23 percent.[29] Appraisers may not think they are showing bias when they assess the value of a home owned by a Black homeowner. In their minds, they may have been taught a community of color is less desirable and, in turn, less valuable. That is why it is so important to have diversity in all levels of positions that affect the future and financial situation for minority communities.

If you are a young white person, your parents may have taught you that Black people are less than you. They may have reinforced that messaging by the way they treated people in the Black community when you saw them outside of your home. That messaging would then reinforce that you should not see them at your level when you grow up and take on a position that allows you to assign a value to their worth. That same bias then affects the position or stature they can take on in business and the value of their home or community. The bias that was taught when you were young

[29] Perry, Andre M., Jonathan Rothwell, and David Harshbarger. "The Devaluation of Assets in Black Neighborhoods." *Brookings*, November 27, 2018. https://www.brookings.edu/research/devaluation-of-assets-in-black-neighborhoods/. Accessed August 22, 2021.

would then transition to the financial viability of the Black community in the future.

Until there is change in this and other financially connected situations, society will continue to operate on that negative path. If people don't assess their bias and try to make changes proactively, these situations will continue to affect Black and brown communities negatively in the future, keeping the minority communities down and undervalued, and hindering their opportunity for growth.

One example of gender bias was recently best described by ESPN showcasing an image of the Greatest Athletes of All Time (GOATs). When the image was released, it only included male athletes—thus making the assumption that when you think of the greatest athletes of all time, you don't think of great female athletes like Serena Williams, Simone Biles, Billie Jean King, Megan Rapinoe, or Jackie Joyner-Kersee. These amazing athletes were left out because of bias. I'm certain that the person (whom I assume is a man) who created that image did not think there was anything wrong because, in his mind, he only sees men as great athletes.

Simone Biles is so good that she has moves in her routine no one has ever landed due to the extreme danger of even attempting them. After her triple-twisting, double somersault during a floor routine at the 2019 U.S. National Championships, the International Gymnastics Federation (FIG) changed the entire scoring system and rules because Simone skews the competition with her talent. When you have an athlete like that, it wouldn't be a stretch to add her name to a conversation about the greatest of all time.

This is just one of many examples of an unconscious bias that affects not just the ability of women or minorities to grow and succeed but also to be seen as equals and to have the opportunity to flourish financially.

Another example that is subtle and yet has the potential to create the largest negative impact for women and minorities is the bias being coded into artificial intelligence

(AI). I remember listening to a TED Talk not too long ago during which a woman named Kriti Sharma mentioned that when people think of unconscious bias, they need to think deeper than just corporate training for staff.[30] Sharma worked for a large tech firm where the majority of the AI programmers were men, and they were inadvertently building bias into everything from apps that review resumes and sort based on preferences to apps for everyday households. Have you ever noticed that when you have to yell out a command, the voice that responds is female, but when a resource offers you information or education, the voice is male?

Common examples show we are using female AI voices in apps like Alexa or Siri that respond to requests and demands, while IBM's male Watson voice is portrayed as a beacon of business expertise and intelligence. An example is when, in 2011, IBM staged a competition for Watson to compete against Ken Jennings on Jeopardy.[31]

In the same TED Talk, Sharma discusses an example of a hiring manager who was trying to find the next tech leader for a company. Sharma says that humans have reinforced their own bias into the AI, which can lead the system to screen out female candidates. A study by *PeerJ Computer Science* analyzed data from GitHub, a San Francisco-based, open-source software community, which is the largest host of source code in the world. According to the study, code written by women was accepted 78.6 percent of the time

---

[30] Sharma, Kriti. "How to Keep Human Bias out of AI." *TED Talks*, March 2018. https://www.ted.com/talks/kriti_sharma_how_to_keep_human_bias_out_of_ai?language=en.

[31] Walsh, Bryan. "Looking Back at Watson's 2011 'Jeopardy!' Win." *Axios*, February 13, 2021. https://www.axios.com/ibm-watson-jeopardy-win-language-processing-8248ddd1-4281-4d48-b23c-453d07555c66.html. Accessed August 22, 2021.

when their gender was unknown.[32] This was 4 percent higher than the acceptance rate for men. However, when the submitter's gender was known to be female, the code was only accepted 62.5 percent of the time. The solution is not to encourage women to hide their identity. The solution must be to remove bias from the equation.

When companies use AI for job placement, bias from the past gets embedded into your selections for the future. They've built the technology to study companies' patterns of behavior and the type of people hiring managers prefer for a given job. They study what type of people are currently in each role. So if a position has a history of men from a certain university with a certain skill set, the app will find you more people just like them.

The Washington Post had an article about an app for kids that didn't include Black hairstyles in the avatar options. There was a young girl who was working hard to earn enough points on the app to create her avatar.[33] When she finally earned her points, she went into the avatar options and did not find any hairstyles that matched her African American hairstyle. She wrote to the company, and they actually responded. They answered the young girl's request and also made updates to accommodate head coverings for those children who don't show their hair and wheelchair options.

---

[32] Terrell, Josh, Andrew Kofink, Justin Middleton, Clarissa Rainear, Emerson Murphy-Hill, Chris Parnin, and Jon Stallings. 2017. "Gender differences and bias in open source: pull request acceptance of women versus men." *PeerJ Computer Science*, May 1, 2017. https://peerj.com/articles/cs-111/. Accessed August 22, 2021.

[33] Page, Sydney. "This 7-Year-Old Persuaded an Educational App to Include 'Black-Girl Hair' like Hers." *The Washington Post*, May 5, 2021. http://www-washingtonpost-com.cdn.ampproject.org/c/s/www.washingtonpost.com/lifestyle/2021/05/05/freckle-app-black-girl-hair/?outputType=amp. Accessed August 22, 2021.

There are so many stories of inclusivity. The importance of having diversity in your staff and at the highest levels of your organization is because there are so many decisions that impact a diverse community. When designing AI apps, if you do not have diverse voices providing input into layout and creation, you will most likely exclude the true community of customers that you're trying to reach.

These are just a few examples of the importance of recognizing unconscious bias. They reinforce the importance of developing solutions that are embedded deep into the company culture. At the end of the day, we all have an opportunity to develop solutions and learn from mistakes of the past.

I believe the biggest failure in not recognizing our unconscious bias is that we often forget how that bias can impact someone's financial future. When a board of directors made up of only white men looks around the table, they might not see anything wrong with the fact that everyone at the table is of the same race and gender. This is an ongoing issue. It not only affects the financial future of the women and minorities who were left off the board, but also the financial success of the company that lacks diversity of thought on their board.

I personally define unconscious bias as things you don't think about, but that impact how you interact with people every day. Sometimes it is as simple as a woman walking down the street. When she sees a man walking toward her, she might clutch her purse tighter or switch to the other side of the street. Why is the woman showing signs of concern? Is it because a man is walking toward her? As the reader of this story, how would you describe the woman and the man? I would assume that depending on your race and gender, you will describe the look of the characters and the reasons for the woman's change in behavior differently.

We will all describe the story in a different way because of our own personal experiences. You, as the reader, will make your own determination based on your own perspective. Our stories shape our lives. They shape our actions, our reactions, and our thoughts. As a woman in the business world, I have had a variety of experiences that no man would understand because he's not a woman. But if I told those stories to other women, they would shake their heads, nod, and share a similar story. As an African American woman and CEO, it's harder for me to find a lot of heads nodding in understanding because the percentage of African American women in CEO positions is much smaller than when I was a manager, director, or VP.

Diversity of thought is important to shape positive outcomes in business decisions, but that diversity of thought should come from a diverse group of people. I think about that every time I see an organization highlight a diversity session at a conference with no minorities on the panel—or when only white men and women are nominated for a diversity and inclusion award.

What is an Ally?

I recently spoke with a friend who shared a conversation she had with an industry leader we'll call Andrea. Andrea asked about my friend's experience at work as a person of color. Andrea was curious if my friend felt included in leadership opportunities and also asked about the experiences of other people of color. My friend shared her open and honest opinion. She said she didn't always feel her voice was being heard. Also, many of her Black friends mentioned that when they were given a promotion, they sometimes felt they were selected because management needed to check a box. When they shared their ideas on strategy or growth, their ideas were often not acted upon—or else they were not listened to at all.

Andrea listened to my friend and then said she and her friends must be thinking wrong. Andrea was sure people of color were supported and didn't believe management would hire someone just to check a box. It is unfortunate that often, unless a person has directly experienced a specific type of bias, they do not understand when someone who has experienced it shares their concerns. It seems to be a part of human nature to be oblivious to bias when you are not a target of it. Andrea had specifically asked to be an ally to my friend, but when given the opportunity to listen and provide support, Andrea doubted my friend's story.

HOW TO BE AN ALLY

WHEN SOMEONE SHARES A RACIST EXPERIENCE WITH YOU

(TIPS BY MITA MALLICK: HEAD OF INCLUSION,
EQUITY AND IMPACT AT CARTA)

1. Begin by hearing them and believing them.
2. Never minimize or dismiss what they are sharing.
3. Understand that it's not your job to be an investigative reporter. Simply let them share their story and experience.
4. Use supportive language such as, "thank you for trusting me and sharing."
5. Continue to check in and let them know you are available should they need it.

Like Andrea, when an individual confides their trust and shares a racist experience that they themselves encounter, we have the opportunity to learn how to become a true friend and ally:

The Real Champion

Another friend was approached by a leader in her industry who offered to be her champion. The leader admitted she had recently taken some diversity and inclusion training and felt compelled to give back to a woman of color by highlighting her value and worth. This friend asked for my thoughts and advice on how she should respond to the woman who was offering to support her. I told her the following story of how I would truly define a champion.

A few years ago, I met a gentleman named Marc. Marc was the Chief Operations Officer at a mid-sized association and he was thinking of creating a new Chief Marketing Officer (CMO) position at his company. His goal was to find someone he could rely upon to run his marketing operations and grow all areas of marketing and sales. He asked for my advice on what qualities he should search for and where to find someone to fill this role. I told him the ins and outs of my success in the C-suite and spent a great deal of time explaining some of the challenges I had experienced as a CMO. I wanted to be transparent and ensure the person he hired would be positioned for success.

The unusual thing about leading marketing efforts is that, for some reason, everyone has an opinion about the topic. Sitting around the leadership table, if our chief economist provided his input on the status of the economy and the position he would like the organization to take, everyone would nod their head in agreement. The same would happen with our attorney. When he presented his opinion on a legal situation, everyone agreed. But when I advised on our marketing strategy and proposed plans for moving forward, people would often say, "Well, actually I think we should do XYZ." I reminded Marc of the importance of trusting the people you put into a leadership role and allowing them to exhibit their expertise. Just remember who you are paying to perform each role.

He said, "Wow, you're amazing! How do I hire somebody like you?" At the end of the day, I went back to my job feeling flattered and thought nothing more about the conversation. A month later, to my surprise, I received phone calls from five different headhunters, all of whom mentioned I had been recommended to them by Marc. As I participated in these conversations, it turned out that the jobs they were discussing were not for the next CMO or COO, but rather at the CEO level.

At the time, I had no intention of leaving my job and gave zero implication that was my desire, but Marc felt it was important to make a broader collection of individuals aware of my existence in the space. A real champion doesn't just *say* he or she wants to be your champion. Real champions take action by going out of their way to share their knowledge of you and your skills and build you up within an organization or industry.

Be the Champion

For those of you who are interested in being someone's champion, that's great! It is always important to share someone's success, especially when he or she may not be seen by a broader spectrum of people. You can champion someone within your company or someone within your industry. Everyone needs an unbiased voice to celebrate them, especially women and minorities who do not dominate the majority of leadership roles. Here are three tips or strategies to help others grow:

- When you meet talented people, tell others about their greatness.
- Share networking events or other opportunities with up-and-coming stars in your space.
- Be humble. Providing access and opportunity is a reward in and of itself.

Find Your Champion

It is important to have a champion in your professional life—someone who supports you, encourages you, and shares your greatness with others in the professional community. I have been blessed with some wonderful champions in my career and I am grateful for their support and encouragement over the years. If you are in search of a champion, there are many ways to find one. No matter what profession you are in, I am certain there is an association that represents your industry. Many people find supporters through membership and participation in an association. Associations provide a person with education, thought leadership, and networking opportunities that grow your knowledge, experience, and professional circle. Through those groups, you may also be able to join a council or committee and gain additional experience and leadership opportunities. When seeking out a champion through those groups in your current work environment or other spaces, always remember these three strategies:

- Be open
- Be receptive
- Be humble

As individuals, we should all work to assess our responses to others' opinions, especially in the work environment. Established companies often fail to innovate because they don't listen to fresh perspectives that can be brought forward by younger members of the team. In addition to trying to listen, we must also explore some of the unconscious reasons why we discount other's opinions.

Have you ever been a part of a committee that was interviewing senior-level executives for a role? Or maybe you have participated as a part of a committee that was deciding upon the qualifications of an applicant? Often, bias occurs even in what appears to be the most positive ways. An example I would offer is how you define the attributes of a person you interviewed. Often, non-minorities will define minorities in different ways. I offer as an example a line Chris Rock would often say in his stand-up routine. He once talked about how everyone always described Colin Powell as well spoken. Of course he's well spoken; he's a college educated man. But the mindset was that white Americans were so amazed to hear a Black man speak intelligently.

Think about what people experience in everyday activities. I was flying with my daughter and husband not so long ago and were so happy to receive an upgrade to first class (best use of miles with a child, for sure). On a U.S. domestic flight, the first-class seating format is normally two and two. My daughter and I were on one side of the aircraft and my husband was across the aisle, sitting next to a stranger. When we took our seats, I noticed the woman seated next to my husband was African American. My own personal experience made me wonder if they would assume the other woman was with my husband instead of me. Sure enough, the woman next to him dozed off and the flight attendant asked my husband if the stranger sitting next to him wanted anything to drink. Then he had to tell the flight attendant that he was not traveling with that woman.

Now, understand this also happens when seated in coach. I remember many flights when, if the random stranger seated next to me was of the same race, the flight attendant often asked if we were together. I have never been asked that when flying seated next to someone of a different race, even when we were traveling together. I have also watched that same situation occur when two Asian people were sitting next to each other. But what's interesting is that I have never heard any of my white friends talk about how the flight attendant assumed they were traveling with the person sitting next to them who happened to be of the same race. Again, it's these little biases that shape someone's experience.

Mellody Hobson of Ariel Investments said in her TED Talk that we need to be comfortable about being uncomfortable when talking about race.[34] "We cannot

[34] Hobson, Mellody. "Color Blind or Color Brave?" *TED Talks*, March 2014. https://www.ted.com/talks/mellody_hobson_color_blind_or_color_brave?language=en. Accessed August 22, 2021.

afford to be color blind," she said. "We must be color brave." Remember, we as individuals must be intentional about including people who don't look like us in our environment. We must include people who don't look or think like us in our social circles and in our work teams. In the end, we will all become better co-workers, friends, and allies.

The Present Looks Very Bright

Organizations often think they're untouchable, but as technology continues to impact business and industries all around the world, change happens fast. According to the article, "Hubris and Late Fees Doomed Blockbuster," during the year 2000, Blockbuster collected nearly $800 million in late fees, accounting for 16 percent of its revenue.[35] When late fees are your golden goose, it's hard for people to think about instituting any kind of change that would affect that revenue. Netflix initially gained customer share because the company did not charge late fees. But by the time Blockbuster recognized the threat to their business and dropped their late fees, it was too late. I can only share what I read about businesses and what appears to be failed strategies. However, I share that example simply to remind business leaders that it is essential to listen to voices below the executive conference table. Other people within the organization might have a different perspective and help the organization be proactive instead of reactive when adjusting to future trends.

Fear of Change

---

[35] Anderson, Mae, and Michael Liedtke. "Hubris–and late fees— doomed Blockbuster." *NBC Universal News Group*, September 23, 2010. https://www.nbcnews.com/id/wbna39332696. Accessed August 22, 2021.

So many companies ignore the ideas of younger generations, when really all they're doing is telling you to think differently and accept change. It can be natural for individuals to fear change, especially if their methods helped them achieve a large measure of success, but those fears and biases cost companies every year.

A Culture That Does Not Allow Room for Failure

All great innovations come through trial and error. I recommend encouraging a culture that does not make people fearful of failure. Try having listening sessions with a broad perspective of employees and fostering a culture that supports ideas that come from any member of the team.

Underestimating Someone's Experience

Sara Blakely had an idea for a different type of hosiery. She found a list of U.S. manufacturers and called them for over a period of six months, only to hear "no" over and over. When working to secure a patent, a lawyer thought Blakely's idea was so bad that she must have been sent by the TV show *Candid Camera* as a prank. Needless to say, she persisted and her idea—Spanx—made her the youngest female self-made billionaire in history.[36] Blakely was finding it hard to break through in an industry in which, as she says, "The people

---

[36] Zoe Segal, Gillian. "This Self-Made Billionaire Failed the LSAT Twice, Then Sold Fax Machines for 7 Years before Hitting Big-Here's How She Got There." *CNBC*, April 3, 2019. https://www.cnbc.com/2019/04/03/self-made-billionaire-spanx-founder-sara-blakely-sold-fax-machines-before-making-it-big.html. Accessed August 22, 2021.

who were making [undergarments] were not spending all day in them."

How often do we look at someone who is younger and discount their ideas for their lack of experience? It's not just the 50-year-old who looks at the 30-year-old and says, "What do they know?" but also the 30-year-old, who looks at the 15-year-old and says the same. Ideas are born of the way we see the world and we must acknowledge the simple truth that the overwhelming majority of the latest innovations in this country were built by someone who was not taken seriously by a member of an older generation.

New ideas should not be seen as a threat to established industry, but as a way to build on established practices and make them better. While the drive for innovation may come from one area, the knowledge of best practices may come from another. That combination of knowledge and curiosity can lead us to what works, but before your organization gets there, we have to acknowledge what we do and don't know.

I will never forget, at one of my previous organizations, talking about the importance of us creating a Facebook page. I was new at the company and they dismissed me and literally said, "There's no way Facebook will have an impact on a national scale." Hindsight proves that comment was correct because Facebook's impact is not national, it's global.

If someone is offering feedback, it should be seen as a gift and not a challenge. We've seen the results when giants like the yellow pages were displaced by Google and taxis were displaced by Uber. How many within an industry stood tall and offered a different perspective?

The only question is *are you listening?*

Summary

- Unconscious bias is taught at a young age, so be aware of the words and stereotypes you express to young people.
- Diversity in leadership drives financial success.
- Bias negatively affects the financial growth of women and minorities.
- Be aware that humans are embedding their own bias into AI, and we need to make sure to avoid that in the future.
- Strive to achieve diversity of thought within a diverse group of people.
- Be a *real* ally or champion.

Where Are You Really From?

As an adopted Korean American from a very rural community, my identity came to me in bits and pieces throughout my life. As one of the few non-white members of the community in which I grew up, I was seen as white. My classmates would ask, "How do your eyes work?" Eventually, everyone just accepted me as white. Later in life, there were side glances and strange looks when I would walk hand-in-hand with my white father. Was I a mail-order bride? Was I a prostitute?

College presented my first experience with a large Asian community. I found myself grouped with other Asians despite my lack of interest in participating. In a freshman writing class, my teaching assistant asked me to help a Japanese student with his writing because English wasn't his first language. It didn't strike me until later that he paired us together because we were both Asian. After all, Asian is Asian, right?

After college, I moved to Baltimore, a city rich in its diversity and with a history of racism. In the Hampden community where I lived, my white neighbors would sometimes lament that the Black students at the local high school were bringing trouble into the neighborhood. "They aren't *our* kids," they would say to me. On the same day, the drug-addicted sex worker who often solicited at the end of our street might yell, "Go back to where you came from," letting me know I wasn't welcome in her town. My Black neighbors would share stories of being *other* with me, knowing I wasn't white, yet diminishing the racism I experienced. They said it wasn't the same.

When I travel, people wonder about my ethnicity. In a market in Charleston, a lovely woman yelled to me across the room, "Do you speak English?" as I browsed the stalls. On a trip with my husband, an older British gentleman asked if he could purchase me when my husband was done. On a girls' outing, a man began speaking to me in Japanese to impress the women I was with. He told me, "I lived in Japan." People assume I teach math, play music, am a doctor, speak English perfectly but also know any number of Asian languages, behave demurely, act as a tiger mom, and make the perfect dumpling— all while quietly supporting my husband and caring for my family, as good Asian women are believed to do. I am both *we* and *they*, depending on a person's mood. I've heard I should be grateful. Asians are the model minority, so when someone asks, "Where are you from...and don't say New Jersey," they think it's a compliment. But it's not a compliment; it's just a reminder that they feel I don't belong. I'm an *us* when it's easy and a *them* when it's not. The qualities that we in the United States look for in strong leaders are hard to see when they are clouded by bias. How do we–the *others*–challenge that in ourselves and others?

—Vicky Schneider, Advancement Professional at Johns Hopkins University

Through the Lens of a Woman

In my thirty-plus years in the construction industry, I've gotten to know two truths quite well:

Women in this industry face a different set of standards than their male counterparts.

The individuals responsible for setting those differing standards are often well-meaning humans who don't even realize they're doing it.

It's not a conscious, malevolent bias that has created an unfair situation. It's an unconscious bias, but the end result is just as unfair.

Why does this happen? I believe it is because there are a lot of individuals who haven't been forced to look at a situation through a viewpoint that's different from their own. That gives them blind spots that lead to workplace inequities. The solution is to put a spotlight on those unconscious biases and encourage more people to put themselves into the shoes of those who might be affected by them.

One of my favorite stories to illustrate this kind of unconscious bias involves a married couple I hired years ago. The wife was a senior person who had hard-to-find skills and experience our team needed. Her husband was trainable to fill another role we needed, so we hired them both and put them in the field. She was doing a great job and was quickly promoted to Project Engineer, and he was a quick learner who had become a valued employee as well.

They were in their early thirties and getting ready to start a family. When the wife got pregnant with their first child, she started getting everything squared away–the daycare, the drop-off and pickup schedule, everything. Toward the end of her pregnancy, I had a vacation planned. When I got back, she came to me completely upset. It turned out that while I was away, the decision was made to send her husband to a remote location where it was no longer possible for him to commute, making it impossible for him to be home to do his part in caring for the baby. She was devastated about what that would mean once the baby arrived.

Perplexed, I went to a member of the leadership team to ask for an explanation. I was told in a reassuring tone, "Oh, don't worry, Nancy! She can go on flex time and that way she can figure out how to manage the kid on her own." This man was being completely sincere, but he was missing the point. It wasn't malicious. He just didn't see it from the expectant family's perspective.

So I asked him, "Why don't we let her husband have flex time instead?"

"We would never do that."

Dumbfounded, I asked, "And why is that?"

His response was priceless, "Well, Nancy–men can't breastfeed!"

I could hardly believe the words coming out of this well-meaning man's mouth. So I said to him, "Oh, so what you're telling me is my ability to breastfeed and my career–those two facts are attached to each other. Is that what you're saying? Tell me something, who is the primary breadwinner in that relationship?"

He paused, like this thought hadn't occurred to him, and finally answered, "She is."

So I said to him, "Here's my deal. They might choose to do exactly what you're suggesting, but that should be their choice. We shouldn't make that choice for them."

Immediately, he said, "You're absolutely right! I got that all wrong. I can't believe I did that!"

And at that moment, it clicked for him. He was able to see the situation from a perspective other than his own worldview. I didn't blame this man one bit. He simply hadn't had the opportunity to look through a woman's lenses before. When you bring a different viewpoint to a person's attention, they can see through different lenses. This is why diversity is so important, so we can see beyond our unconscious biases.

—Nancy Novak, Chief Innovation Officer, Compass Datacenters

IT'S ALL ABOUT THE LAWS

> "I'm sometimes asked, 'When will there be enough [women on the Supreme Court]'? And I say, 'When there are nine.' People are shocked. But there'd been nine men, and nobody's ever raised a question about that."
> —Supreme Court Justice Ruth Bader Ginsburg (RBG)

On January 10, 1878, Senator Aaron Sargent (R-CA) introduced a Senate resolution that provided for women's suffrage. The language of that resolution reads: "The right of citizens of the United States to vote shall not be denied or abridged by the United States or by any State on account of sex." If that language looks familiar to you, it should. It's the language that was used verbatim in the 19th Amendment, which was adopted in 1920 and allows for voting rights for women.

It is a footnote in history that is not often discussed in detail, but the 19th Amendment was originally proposed as the 16th Amendment, which was nicknamed the Susan B. Anthony Amendment. However, the resolution was put on the back burner and defeated many times until, more than four decades later, it finally passed. The majority of the political sentiment was against allowing women to vote, as summarized during debate that took place during the amendment when it was originally proposed.

- "It would be unjust to impose the heavy burden of governing, which so many men seek to evade, on the great mass of women who do not wish for it, to gratify the few who do."[37]
- "These voters will be inexperienced in public affairs."[38]
- "Very few of them wish to assume the irksome and responsible duties which this measure thrusts upon them."[39]

Early in my career, after my work efforts doubled my company's income, I received numerous compliments from leadership. But when I asked to be compensated appropriately for those results, a manager actually said he didn't understand why I needed the money when I am a single woman. The idea that women were being protected from the messy job of leadership still persists today and it runs rampant throughout our legal system.

In a society that requires two incomes to stay above water, it is important that we re-evaluate all laws and policies that may affect families or gender. Many laws were written with the expectation that women stay home with the children while men go to work. One example of a trailblazer who

---

[37] Hoar, George Frisbie, John H. Mitchell, and Angus Cameron. "Woman Suffrage in the U.S. Senate, 1879: Argument for a Sixteenth Amendment," Image 4. *Library of Congress*, www.loc.gov/resource/rbnawsa.n8360/?sp=4&st=text. Accessed August 22, 2021.

[38] Hoar.

[39] Hoar.

worked to fight against gender discrimination was Ruth Bader Ginsburg, who spent a lot of her career defending men who were unfairly discriminated against because of these laws.

Upon her death in late 2020, many reflected on RBG's career and re-discovered the critical role she played in gender equality. As a young lawyer, RBG argued in front of the Supreme Court on behalf of a man named Leon Goldfarb. Goldfarb had applied for Social Security survivors benefits after his wife Hannah passed away but was denied. Even though Mrs. Goldfarb had paid Social Security taxes for 25 years, her husband was not considered eligible unless he was receiving half of his support from her at her time of death. Since the law did not enforce this same requirement on widows, the court determined this violated the Due Process Clause of the Fifth Amendment and Mr. Goldfarb was unfairly discriminated against because of his gender.

Ginsburg discovered that this strategy was particularly effective with the all-male judges she was arguing in front of. She made a point to argue that if these laws were discriminating against men, then the basis for the law was inherently unfair. Here are a few other examples from Ginsburg's arguments before the Supreme Court:[40]

- Stephen Wiesenfeld, who decided to cut back his work hours to care for his newborn son after his wife Paula died in childbirth.[41] The law permitted widows to collect special benefits while caring for minor children, but not widowers.
- Sharron Frontiero, a United States Air Force lieutenant, sought a dependent's allowance for

---

[40] "Ruth Bader Ginsburg: A Reading List." *The Library at Washington and Lee University School of Law*. A list of Ruth Bader Ginsburg's arguments before the Supreme Court is available at https://libguides.wlu.edu/law/RBG/arguments. Accessed August 22, 2021.

[41] Weinberger v. Wiesenfeld, 420 U.S. 636 (1975).

her husband. [42] Federal law stipulated that military wives automatically became dependents, but husbands of female members of the military were not accepted unless they were dependent on their wives for over one-half of their support.

- Widower Mel Kahn applied for a property tax exemption after his wife passed away.[43] This exemption was written for widows who had recently lost their husbands and, therefore, Kahn was denied because of his gender. He sued and a circuit court held that the statute was gender-based and, therefore, violated the Equal Protection Clause of the Fourteenth Amendment.

RBG leveraged the concept that unequal treatment anywhere was unfair and her unique method was to identify key cases that negatively impacted men. This opened up the idea for a nation that did not always view discrimination through this lens that this form of hypocrisy should not be faced by anyone. Equal protection under the law reinforces why it is important to have more balance in diversity, equity, and inclusion in the courts. This is especially so with states like California passing landmark legislation requiring public companies that have their executive base in the state to have at least three women on their boards by the end of 2021. California became the first state to address the problem of inequality on executive boards through legislation, but there is still a long way to go.

According to the Federal Judicial Center, more than 73 percent of sitting federal judges are men and 80 percent are white.[44] If the goals of the justice system are to provide equal rights and justice, it is imperative we provide a structure by

---

[42] Frontiero v. Richardson, 411 US 677 (1973).

[43] Kahn v. Shevin, 416 US 351 (1974).

[44] "Demography of Article III Judges, 1789-2020." *Federal Judicial Center*. www.fjc.gov/history/exhibits/graphs-and-maps/race-and-ethnicity. Accessed August 22, 2021.

which people of all backgrounds have legal and structural access across the highest positions within this system.

A 2020 report by the Alliance for Board Diversity and Deloitte found that among Fortune 500 companies, women held about 26.5 percent of board seats and minority women just 5.7 percent.[45] In this modern era, the phrases "the first female" and "the first minority female in a leadership role" are still newsworthy, but we should be asking ourselves why it is just now occurring for the first time. While seeing a female American vice president for the first time in history is an indicator of progress, the fact that we still have to single out, celebrate, and point out when a woman achieves at a high level means we've been moving at much too slow of a pace.

The Impossible Qualification

I recently watched Amazon founder Jeff Bezos launch a rocket into space with his new aerospace company Blue Origin. Included in his select team was 82-year-old Wally Funk, who became the oldest person to go into space. As I listened to the story, I learned that Wally Funk was one of the women from the 1960s First Lady Astronaut Trainees (FLATS) program, more commonly known as Mercury 13.[46] In this story, they discussed that the women of Mercury 13 went through the same strenuous exams as the men training for space and not only met, but often surpassed, the results of the men. However, the women could not become astronauts because

---

[45] "Missing Pieces Report: The Board Diversity Census of Women and Minorities on Fortune 500 Boards, 6th edition." Deloitte. *Alliance for Board Diversity.* http://www2.deloitte.com/us/en/pages/center-for-board-effectiveness/articles/missing-pieces-board-diversity-census-fortune-500-sixth-edition.html. Accessed August 22, 2021.

[46] Miller, Michelle. *CBS This Morning*, July 20, 2021.

NASA required them to be military test pilots and the military at that time did not allow women to fly.

This story intrigued me, as I was in the middle of writing this book and I wanted to learn a little more. It made me think about this chapter and the laws from the 1960s. I discovered that Mercury 13 was privately funded by Jacqueline Cochran, who was a pilot and pioneer in women's aviation. The women were trained by Dr. William Lovelace, an aerospace physician and the head of NASA's committee on life science. However, Dr. Lovelace was unable to complete the third phase of testing, which involved space simulation, because he needed access to military facilities. "[T]he government would not allow Lovelace to use military equipment for testing women when NASA had no intention of sending them to space, or even considering women as astronaut candidates at the time. As a result, the FLATs program was canceled."[47]

Every time I hear these types of stories, I am amazed that women have gotten as far as they have. There have been and continue to be so many impossible qualifications, all which are controlled by men, that continue to tie our hands and keep us from achieving equality. We all must work together to break down these barriers that continue to hold women back from achieving the highest levels of success.

A Vision for Workplace Parenting and Culture

In my first year as CEO, I'll never forget being notified of the passage of the District of Columbia paid Family Leave Act,

---

[47] Krishna, Swapna. "The Mercury 13: The Women Who Could Have Been NASA's First Female Astronauts." Space.com. *Space*, July 24, 2020. https://www.space.com/mercury-13.html. Accessed August 22, 2021.

which allowed for a specific number of months of leave for both a new mother *and* a new father. When I read through the first draft of the document, I noticed there were several references to "she" versus "he or she." While this was changed in an updated version, even today, people still have the unconscious bias to write in female terminology as it relates to family leave.

Years ago, I spoke with a co-worker whose wife was expecting soon. When I asked how much time he was going to take off when the baby was born, he said he didn't feel comfortable asking his boss to take more than a couple of days. He said he had accrued the time but felt pressured to return to work while his wife was home. It seems like so many categorize the birth of a child as a women's issue, as if it has no impact on men. But in households of all kinds, paid family leave is essential to bond as a family during this delicate time with a new child.

A study from the University of Michigan and University of California, San Diego talks about the changing career trajectories of new parents in STEM.[48] The report indicates that 43 percent of women leave full-time STEM employment after the birth of their first child while only 23 percent of new fathers leave STEM.

With the tech industry responsible for a significant number of the high-wage jobs in the modern economy, the culture of long hours and expectations for working weekends may not be the most parent friendly.

A recent UNICEF study compared 41 developed countries and found the U.S. came in dead last in terms of

---

[48] Cech, Erin A., and Mary Blair-Loy. "The Changing Career Trajectories of New Parents in STEM." *Proceedings of the National Academy of Sciences of the United States of America*, March 5, 2019. https://doi.org/10.1073/pnas.1810862116. Accessed August 22, 2021.

paid leave available to mothers and fathers.[49] The U.S. is the only high-income country, as classified by the World Bank, that offers zero federally mandated weeks of paid maternity leave.[50] At the time of this writing, out of 193 countries in the United Nations, only New Guinea, Suriname, a few South Pacific Island nations, and the U.S. do not have a national paid parental leave law. The U.S. is the only industrialized nation on that list.

According to the U.S. Census Bureau, in 1976, only 56.3 percent of married mothers worked for pay compared to 69.6 percent in 2017.[51] Despite the increase in mothers taking a role in providing income for the family, time and again, after a new child is born, the extended absence frequently has long-term implications for her career. The McKinsey Lean-In "broken rung" data reveals that men end up with 62 percent of manager jobs while women hold just 38 percent.[52] This disparity is not solely because of lack of knowledge, ability, or skill, but because many of those first promotions are missed because of qualified women having a child at the time that they might have been promoted. Qualified and capable women having children should not serve as a career-defining penalty that impacts future promotions exponentially. We strive for and seek equality,

---

[49] Ferrante, Mary Beth. "UNICEF Study Confirms: The U.S. Ranks Last for Family-Friendly Policies." *Forbes*, June 21, 2019. http://www.forbes.com/sites/marybethferrante/2019/06/21/unicef-study-confirms-the-u-s-ranks-last-for-family-friendly-policies/. Accessed August 22, 2021.

[50] Hernandez, Dominic. "Fast Facts: Maternity Leave Policies Across the Globe." Vital Record. *Texas A&M Health*, July 26, 2018. https://vitalrecord.tamhsc.edu/fast-facts-maternity-leave-policies-across-globe/. Accessed August 22, 2021.

[51] "Table F-14. Work Experience of Husband and Wife--Married-Couple Families, by Presence of Children Under 18 Years Old and by Median and Mean Income." *U.S. Census Bureau*. http://www.census.gov/data/tables/time-series/demo/income-poverty/historical-income-families.html. Accessed August 22, 2021.

52 McKinsey & Company. 2019.

but what happens if the laws don't allow it? We need universal family leave in the United States.

Conservatorship—A Case Study

Take a moment to think of any male celebrity who has struggled with some type of addiction. Has this celebrity gone into a rehab facility to address issues? Have they been arrested or taken a mug shot? Have they been caught on video saying or doing something unflattering?

Now that you've thought about it. Ask yourself, how many of them have had their finances put into a conservatorship? And I ask this question as food for thought. If they were temporarily put into a conservatorship with their mother having control, how long do you think the courts would require that to stay in place? According to the Superior Court of California, a conservatorship is a legal concept in the United States which allows a judge to grant one or more guardians control over an individual's finances when that person is physically or mentally unable to manage them on their own.[53]

Let's turn to the more specific example of Britney Spears, who has been in the news about her conservatorship. Spears' finances were placed into a temporary conservatorship with her father when she was 27 years old. However, after more than 13 years, several albums and tours, a Las Vegas residency, a new perfume and clothing line, and much success, her father still controls her finances. At the time of this writing, every request to the courts to remove it has been denied, spurring the #FreeBritney movement.

---

[53] "About Probate Conservatorships." *The Superior Court of California, County of Santa Clara.* https://www.scscourt.org/self_help/probate/conservatorship/conservatorship_overview.shtml. Accessed August 22, 2021.

While there have certainly been a variety of high-profile male celebrities and musicians who have undergone conservatorship, many of these cases were put in place just prior to their deaths or because of very serious medical issues. Rarely have these cases been put in place for someone so young, and almost never permanently. I bring this up purely as food for thought as just another example of how differently women are treated. The conversation I want people to have is this: just be more aware of the differences between how women's lives may be affected, managed, or perceived as compared to men's.

Wage Gap Crisis

The Lilly Ledbetter Fair Pay Act of 2009 is a critical law that amends the Civil Rights Act of 1964 and states that the statute of limitations for filing an equal-pay lawsuit resets with each new paycheck affected by that discriminatory action. This law is essential since employees often go months or years without realizing the pay disparity in their role. While this act allows women to have protection for when they are underpaid in a role that is comparable to the job they already have, it does not address the disparity that exists because of the unequal female representation on boards and in the C-suite. How can you sue for a role you never received because you were never given the opportunity to get there? This is more widespread than the United States. We are finding countries like Iceland and Sweden have listed that all companies are required to have equal pay and women in leadership by 2022.

Though laws may lag, in many cases, there are steps private industry can take. For example, Goldman Sachs will no longer do IPOs for companies with all-male boards.[54] This is an example of the private sector leveraging access to influence positive change.

This change is more essential than ever as the pandemic led us to discover the gender disparity that can be experienced in a crisis.[55] Many women called the pandemic-related recession a *shecession*, as schools closed and many business and restaurants in service industry related jobs closed their doors. Women faced a great deal of pain and frustration, and it highlighted that when things get messy, it should not just be on women to bear the increased brunt of the caregiving. But for companies, taking care of women is so much more than just a *nice-to-have*. Having women play decision-making roles in your company has been proven to be profitable. In exchange for a broad level of expertise, it shouldn't be a stretch to provide a few weeks of recovery time during an employee's tenure. When people work in teams and play to their strengths, a company can be more effective. Having people from a variety of backgrounds enhances the overall abilities and talents of the organization. It's essential we consider this within the workplace culture. While the Family and Medical Leave Act protects those who need to take time off to take care of a newborn child or for medical conditions, it only allows for three months of unpaid medical leave.

---

[54] Elsesser, Kim. "Goldman Sachs Won't Take Companies Public If They Have All-Male Corporate Boards." *Forbes*, January 23, 2020. https://www.forbes.com/sites/kimelsesser/2020/01/23/goldman-sachs-wont-take-companies-public-if-they-have-all-male-corporate-boards/. Accessed August 22, 2021.

[55] Laughlin, Lynda, and Megan Wisniewski. "Women Represent Majority of Workers in Several Essential Occupations." *U.S. Census Bureau*, March 23, 2021. http://www.census.gov/library/stories/2021/03/unequally-essential-women-and-gender-pay-gap-during-covid-19.html. Accessed August 22, 2021.

I often think of the case of the U.S. Women's National Soccer Team, who sued for equal pay only to have Federal Judge R. Gary Klausner reject the women's team's argument over receiving lower pay than the U.S. men's team.[56] The women's soccer team's fight for equal play drew national news. They were internationally recognized as World Cup champions and had a dominant run of three straight Olympic gold medals, but still were paid less than the men's national team at the time of the lawsuit. It did not matter that the men failed to qualify for consecutive World Cup tournaments and have failed to qualify for three Olympic games in a row. This is another example of gender pay inequity with the decision in the hands of a man.

This brings me back to the ratification of the 19th Amendment. If you were to look at history and think about the Susan B. Anthony Amendment, you may not make the connection that Anthony was born in 1820 and passed away in 1906. She, along with Elizabeth Cady Stanton (who died in 1902), spent their entire lives fighting for something they never got to see adopted. However, they inspired the next generation of leaders to take up the fight, which proved to the world that their work was not in vain.

Today, countless mothers, sisters, students, politicians, activists, actresses, CEOs, and so many more are fighting tooth and nail to put more and more cracks in a glass ceiling that has sometimes seemed less like glass and more like steel, but that does not mean their efforts are not making a difference. We can't predict the day when that glass will shatter, and maybe it won't be within the timeframe we expect; but in the mean-time, every shard that falls to

---

[56] Cater, Franklyn. "Federal Judge Dismisses U.S. Women's Soccer Team's Equal Pay Claim." *NPR*, May 2, 2020. https://www.npr.org/2020/05/02/849492863/federal-judge-dismisses-u-s-womens-soccer-team-s-equal-pay-claim. Accessed August 22, 2021.

the ground represents a new beginning for one person, one family, one company, or maybe even one generation. In Japan, broken objects are often repaired with gold in a technique known as *kintsugi*. The flaw is seen to add to its beauty as it becomes a distinctive part of the object's history. I often think about the repurposing of things that are broken in the essence that they can become far more unique than the originals. The fight to shatter this ceiling should be a call for unity.

Flawed systems can be repurposed and repaired to create something meaningful. Working to provide the full rights and privileges of each and every citizen, equal protection under the law, and realizing a more equitable world for the next generation honors the countless suffragettes of the past who got us to this moment in history in which we can lean on each other, provide resources, sisterhood, and support, and give each other critical reminders to never get their coffee.

Summary

- Much of Ruth Bader Ginsburg's success in gaining equality for women came from her showing how laws discriminated against men.
- California became the first state to address the problem of inequality on executive boards through legislation.
- Study the data that showcases the inequities for gender, so everyone can work to make improvements.
- Building awareness of how women are treated differently in the eyes of the law will help force tough conversations and decrease unconscious bias.
- Equal pay for women is an ongoing challenge that requires everyone in the legal system and workplace to work together to improve it.

A Lawyer, Despite My Gender

As a woman who has worked for over a decade in the male-dominated legal industry, I can attest that traditional notions of men in decision-making roles, gender-based office roles, and pay disparity are ever present. Not only did this create an atmosphere of a good ol' boys' club, but it created a playing field for me uneven to that of my male associates.

The partners at my firms predominantly were male, as is the norm at most law firms. I experienced the effect of this norm early on when I began meeting with clients and showing up for depositions. The assumption by opposing counsel or clients was that I was the paralegal, and that the attorney would show up shortly. It was clear that my presence alone didn't demand the respect normally bestowed upon a lawyer, and that was *because of my gender*.

Knowing I had to work hard to prove myself, I recall desperately trying to make a name and reputation for myself as a sharp, competent litigator, *despite my gender*. I thought I could accomplish this by being good at researching, writing, and crafting legal arguments to advocate for my clients. However, many times, I was forced to balance my substantive and billable work with tasks that were historically considered "women's work" just because I was a woman. Though many, the examples that have stuck with me to this day include:

- Being asked by a male partner to make one of our clients a sandwich. He did not ask me to conduct research related to this client's defense, nor assist with drafting any pleadings, but instead he expected me to utilize my inherent skills as a caregiver and make the client a sandwich. The notion that my sandwich-making skills, not my legal skills, were what I could contribute to this client was deflating at best.

- Being asked by a senior male associate to do tasks that would traditionally be delegated to the most junior attorney on the case. These tasks included printing, making photocopies, and scheduling meetings. At the time, the most junior attorney on our cases was male.
- Being asked to attend client dinners because the client liked blondes.
- Being asked to attend court hearings in front of male judges, not to do anything substantive, but as "eye candy."
- Being expected and asked to spend non-billable time coordinating office holiday lunches and other employees' special occasions. Male counterparts were rarely asked to take time away from substantive work to ensure the conference room was properly set up or cleaned after a shower or retirement party.
- Being asked to attend late night "working dinners" with a senior male associate, which usually involved drinking wine without much work discussion.

Requests such as these were not helping me hone my litigation skills or advance my career. As a young associate working my way up, I knew I had to tread lightly between earning my respect and being insubordinate by saying no. I also knew in my gut that these types of requests were not made of male junior associates. And so one day, to prove my suspicions, I asked one of the male associates if he was ever tasked with sandwich making, scheduling, or making personal photocopies. He, in no uncertain terms, confirmed that he was not. That was as infuriating to me then as it is now.

These may seem like small things to the reader, but they have a real cumulative effect on a young woman's career. If I were to decline these requests, I would not be seen as a team player. Therefore, unlike my male counterparts, I was constantly put in the position of having to spend my time on tasks that had nothing to do with becoming a respected lawyer.

Over the years, I also watched the clear difference between how female and male attorneys are paid and treated when requesting a raise or promotion. For example, during negotiations for employment at one of my jobs, I was advised it was office policy that incoming associates could only request and be approved for a certain salary range. I later learned from a male associate that he was encouraged to request a higher salary range. Similarly, I worked in an office where management encouraged male associates to push for promotions. However, female attorneys were told to wait patiently. Why is it that men are encouraged to be assertive about pay and promotions, while women are essentially given the proverbial pat on the head and told to be patient? This traditional, gender-biased mindset has a direct impact on a woman's earning capacity throughout her career.

Despite all of this, I appreciate the experiences I have had in my career because they helped give me confidence. I learned I didn't need to acquiesce to these ridiculous and unfair requests to earn respect and become a good attorney. The next time a male associate asked me to make him a photocopy, I instead brought him step-by-step instructions on how to print his own emails and copy them. I began turning down the "working dinners" with wine. While pushing back on these requests ultimately created an uncomfortable environment that prompted me to leave that firm, I hope I at least brought attention to the unequal treatment.

—Amanda S., attorney

10

DID YOU MAKE THE ASK?

In a previous role, I managed two people at the same time in similar jobs. What I discovered as I looked into the career trajectory of this man and woman is that he asked for a raise on several occasions while she never made the ask. In her career, she simply took the increase for yearly performance. Years later, when I came into the role, I noticed a major pay disparity between the two of them. As an advocate for equal pay, I immediately worked with the HR department to make the necessary adjustments to realign fairness between those roles and make any other adjustments that were needed on my new team. I always advise both women and men that when you achieve great success in a role, ensure you make the ask. The worst they can say is no.

Now, I'm not saying those who just go to work and do the basic job they're paid to do should be asking for a raise at the end of the year. But if you hit a major milestone, help the company exceed budget by some record amount, or take on new responsibilities, then be sure to assess your worth.

Shark Tank mogul and real estate expert Barbara Corcoran speaks on the topic of fair pay and getting raises often. In a recent article on grow.acorns.com, she says, "Who deserves a raise? It's the person who has taken on more responsibility. Here's what I came in doing, and here's what else I've taken on. That's the argument every boss will respond to."[57]

Anytime I step into my role as a manager, I always assess the diversity of my team and the pay equity. It is amazing to me how many times the variance leans to the side of the men. That is something everyone can try to do when they led a team or influence the pay of another person. Be sure to verify there is equity in the salaries being offered. When I say equity, I mean not just offering someone what you think is right. I am asking you to ensure the scales are balanced to pay the women who are on your team or leading your firm the same amount the market would pay a man to do the same job.

I often think, why is it that when you approach a financial advisor and ask about your portfolio, they tell you the key to long-term financial growth is to diversify? But when you walk into a board room with a monolithic leadership and offer the same advice, people look at you sideways. Diversifying your team is critical to a company's financial success. Forget that it's the right thing to do. It's the profitable thing to do.

"I've been investing now for over ten years on things like Shark Tank deals — and other deals that are brought to me because of Shark Tank—and the majority of my returns come from the companies run by women."
—Kevin O'Leary.

---

[57] Ermey, Ryan. "'If You Want a Raise, You Better Learn How to Ask': Barbara Corcoran's 3 Steps for Getting a Pay Hike." *Grow (Acorns),* April 16, 2021. https://grow.acorns.com/barbara-corcoran-how-to-get-a-raise/. Accessed August 22, 2021.

When people ask about equal access in the C-suite and boardroom, I often cite the above quote by *Shark Tank* investor Kevin O'Leary. On the show, the Sharks invest in business ideas by unpacking their profits, examining their potential, and analyzing their bottom line.

Having a diverse team in leadership isn't a women's issue; it provides bottom-line success for all. A 2019 Credit Suisse study entitled "The CS Gender 3000 in 2019: The changing face of companies" reports that companies that have women in twenty percent or more of their senior management positions generate greater stock performance than companies with less than 15 percent female leadership.[58] When a company increases profits, that return can go to salaries, bonuses, leadership training, shareholders, and a healthier bottom line that will benefit all employees, regardless of gender.

This is all about women and men having the right to choose their own destiny. If she wants to run a company or sit on a board, she should have that option. But there are still structural barriers, biases, and historical legal and social precedents that penalize women who want to be the primary breadwinner in their family. We need to get to a place where there is such equality for men and women that when women are placed in leadership positions, it's no big deal.

How to Make the Ask

Most companies have an annual review process during which management reviews the year and makes note of

---

[58] "The CS Gender 3000 Report 2019. Diversity and Company Performance." *Credit Suisse.* https://www.credit-suisse.com/about-us-news/en/articles/news-and-expertise/cs-gender-3000-report-2019-201910.html. Accessed August 22, 2021.

their high achievers. Many people feel frustrated when they achieve a great deal but aren't recognized. Just keep this in mind:

You have to sell yourself because no one else will.

For those of you who may read this and think, "I already asked, and they said no," I'll mention a statement I say to people all the time:

If it's not in writing, it doesn't exist.

I have often counseled people about the importance of writing reports in business. A report is not just for your boss; it is a reminder to yourself of your milestones and accomplishments throughout the year. Reports are important for your own self-reflection. You should sit back and be proud of the work you're doing and the success you have made in your organization.

Sometimes, we get so busy doing our job, we forget to remember the job we did.

Tips for Writing a Report

- **Numbers don't lie.**
  Be sure to incorporate year-over-year growth, cost savings, and increased revenue if any of those areas tie back to your functions.

- **Get to the point.**
  We can all talk for hours about the importance of what we do; but be sure to be concise about your messaging. You do want someone to read it, and we live in the world of Twitter.

- **Images are everything.**
  You don't need to create an Instagram account to highlight your success, but a picture or a graph can always help guide eyes through a report. The look and feel of the content that is presented will affect the amount of time somebody will spend reviewing it.

Don't Be Afraid to Share the "Humble-Brag"

The *Oxford English Dictionary* defines the humble-brag as "an ostensibly modest or self-deprecating statement with the actual intention of drawing attention to something of which one is proud." When you're taking that confident approach, you're not just doing it for yourself. You're doing it because you want to make a difference and pave the way for the next leader behind you.

I think there are a variety of ways to be humble and confident. The problem is, so much of a woman's confidence is hindered by a mindset in which we are molded to be quiet and receive microaggressions or name-calling for exuding confidence. Remember this simple mantra:

Concern for the perception of your confidence should never be an excuse for hiding it.

There is nothing you can do to prevent someone from having their own perception of your confidence. Worrying about name-calling and someone thinking negatively about you becomes a self-fulfilling prophecy of weakness. They never had to call you a name because you were so afraid of the possibility of what they'd say about you.

Yes, people will call you names behind your back. It may be because they are threatened by your confidence. But their perception should not worry you. The only thing that should worry you is that you may selectively disqualify yourself by never making the ask. Don't worry about what might happen when you throw your hat into the ring, because the only alternative is never to throw your hat into the ring at all. And the possibility of a lost leader who never got a chance out of fear is truly scary. Women need to get into leadership positions and doing so requires them to talk about their accomplishments out loud.

Our individual success should not be treated like a dirty secret. Boldly and proudly share what you have accomplished. It's the only way for people to put you in the role you are destined to be in.

I've Been Promoted, But What Now? Five Strategies for a First-Time Leader

As people in my network are switching to new roles, it made me reflect on what I've learned in my experience as a CEO. I've discovered it's important to gain a few small victories and set a realistic timetable for success. Here are five tips I recommend for anyone in a new position who makes their ask and then rises to a new position.

- **Ask questions and listen.**
  During my first sixty days on the job, I sat down to have one-on-one Q&As with each person on my staff, my board of directors, and the chairs and vice chairs of various committees and councils. I asked them what they enjoyed about their jobs and liked about the organizations, what they would change immediately if they had the power to do so, and where they saw potential for growth. As you arise to next-level roles, it is important to listen and understand those who have been involved in shaping the current organization and take their feedback into account as you set your agenda.
- **Assess all current vendors and contracts.**
  It is standard procedure for a new CEO to review all contractual obligations, banks, insurance, and any other vendors that work with the company. As you rise through the ranks, it can be relevant to familiarize yourself with those existing contracts to understand what the company is currently involved in.
- **Don't get hung up on past failures.**
  It's important to recognize past errors and take those into consideration as you are brainstorming

new ideas. But don't let past failures hinder your potential growth. I learned early in my career that sometimes a company will eliminate a program because it is not successful instead of reviewing the people responsible for making that program a success. Often, people like to tell you about what didn't work in a product, service, or program instead of asking if the right talent was on board for that program to be successful. Ensure you've done a proper assessment of the tools and team needed for your product, service, or program to be a success.

- **Don't be afraid to make the tough decisions**.
  Many people aim to achieve the highest-level position in a company, but oftentimes they forget that being the boss doesn't always mean making friends. There are tough decisions that need to be made for your company to be successful. So, if you are not prepared to take a true assessment of what you need to do the job, then don't go for a job if you're not willing to make all the decisions it requires. People truly appreciate when a leader is willing to make the tough decisions, especially when it's truly for the betterment of the organization.

- **Establish a positive culture**.
  It's important to develop a positive culture within your organization. If you're new to an organization or have been promoted to a leadership role, review your employee handbook and all the rules and processes currently in place. Ask yourself the question: *what makes sense for the future of your company?* Just because you've always done it that way doesn't mean you still need to. When you create a positive culture, you will see the results in the teamwork between your staff and the results of the work they do.

Summary

- Don't be afraid to ask for a raise.
- Managers, be sure there is pay equity between the men and women on your teams.
- Companies with women in leadership are more profitable.
- You have to sell yourself because no one else will.
- If it isn't in writing, it doesn't exist.

Know Your Worth

The average salary for a software trainer is $64,500. My salary is $194,000. Why? Because I asked.

Rarely does one enter a liberal arts arena (teachers, trainers, counselors, non-profits, social workers) with the hopes of making big bucks. Our focus is on the greater good—a mindset that is morally honorable, yet detrimentally disempowering.

For years I justified my salary lot in life with moral statements such as "Well, I love what I do" or "I have a lot of flexibility in this position" or "money isn't everything" while secretly conducting a disempowering seminar in the depths of my brain. I'd tell myself, "The salary range for this job is x—I'd be crazy to ask for more." Even worse, "maybe I'm not really worth x."

Corporate leaders often discuss the importance of being empowered, but what does that mean? According to the *Oxford English Dictionary*, the definition of empowerment is "authority or power given to someone." That is a passive process—one that requires *others* to empower you. May I suggest, instead, that you empower *yourself* by understanding your holistic total worth.

—Audrey Riley-Robinson, Software Trainer, Leidos

11

LEADING AS A WOMAN OF COLOR

I n a previous role, I was hired as a vice president of a large trade association. Within my first week, I met all my direct reports and had a meeting with my whole team. What surprised me was that throughout that week, I also had various people stop by my office to congratulate me for joining the company. They would tell me how excited they were that I had joined the team. Often, they would shake my hand and I felt they looked at me as though they thought I was someone else. There was a look of excitement, as though they might have mistaken me for a famous person. I started to notice those people coming to see me were not part of my team—they were all minorities.

I was the first person of color hired into a VP role in the long history of the company. Minorities from other departments felt compelled to introduce themselves and tell me how happy they were to see a woman of color in a VP role in the organization. It made it very clear that not only did I need to do well in my role for myself, but for the future of other people of color. Believe it or not, there is an unwritten rule that if an organization does not have a history of balanced opportunities for minorities, then there is an expectation that when a minority is hired, they must excel. If not, it is rarely likely they will place another minority in a similar role in the future. So, I felt additional pressure on my shoulders.

Throughout my career, I've managed a variety of industry culture challenges as a young Black female executive in the construction space. From my first role as a manager at a small association to serving as a Chief Marketing Officer for a large one, I've always been the organization's first. As a Black female CEO for an association in the construction space, people have called me a unicorn. But I always felt that there were countless other diverse employees who may have never had the opportunity or access needed to reach my level of success.

I've spent my career representing the construction industry—ninety percent of which is still is made up of white men to this day.[59] I have been in countless rooms where I've heard conversations I wouldn't care to repeat, but I wouldn't be where I am today if I didn't quickly learn tolerance. The ability to recognize the difference between a blatant personal attack and somebody who just truly doesn't recognize that what they're saying is offensive is an important skill. If I responded in an explosive or emotional way to certain comments that are in that gray area of being considered racist or sexist, then I would have struggled to succeed in this industry. My ability to build strong relationships and point out those biases in a non-threatening manner has helped build awareness with far more success than the former response. Positive change requires all of us to work together and provide learning

---

[59] "Women in Construction: The State of the Industry in 2021." BigRentz, Inc. https://www.bigrentz.com/blog/women-construction. Accessed August 22, 2021.

opportunities, rather than using judgment and scrutiny to help people recognize their unconscious bias.

I went to high school in Fairbanks, Alaska. It goes without saying the diversity mix in our northernmost state is not high. However, I truly enjoyed my high school years in one of the friendliest states I've ever lived in. I will never forget the first year I attended Summer Fine Arts Camp at the University of Alaska-Fairbanks. It was a creative program for high schoolers, specializing in music, theater, dance, and the arts. It attracted students from all across the state, including some very rural parts. One day a couple weeks into the program, a guy I had been performing with in the theater production said to me, "You're the first black person I've met—I mean except for at McDonalds or Burger King." Now, many people would immediately fly off the handle over a statement like that that could be perceived as pushing offensive stereotypes about race, but I recognized his intentions. He was trying to say I was very nice, and he was glad he had an opportunity to get to know me—a person who looked different from him. This type of interaction happens every day. You rarely ignore when somebody says something rude, but you should find a way to respond that doesn't make them feel threatened. That will allow them to take your feedback and apply it in the next situation. After hearing his comment, I made a joke in response. Then later, once we got to know each other, I pointed out there's a better way to make that observation in the future.

When I traveled to a vendor meeting with two managers from my team, I couldn't help but notice the almost uncomfortable shock on their faces when we walked in. Had they never had a meeting with three Black women? When I traveled to other vendor meetings with my white male employees, ninety percent of the time, people addressed them as the boss and me as the employee. We were all wearing suits, we were all college-educated, and we all spoke with similar diction and tone. Why the assumption the white male was the head of the department? Was it because that is all they ever saw in leadership roles at the vendor's company?

How do we address this disparity as business leaders? Often, minorities do not believe they will have an opportunity for growth in your company if they do not see someone who looks like them in a leadership role. In addition, people will not believe in minorities who finally attain leadership roles if they have not seen minorities in the highest levels of a company showcasing their success.

The 2020 Racism Awakening

In mid-2020, I spent a lot of time listening and thinking. The tragic death of George Floyd and so many other African Americans by police in this country brings an overwhelming sense of anger and frustration. I am heartbroken every time I hear these stories and frequently reflect on my own shocking experiences of racism throughout my life. There are many people writing about their concerns and frustrations and I, too, have shared mine verbally with my family and friends. But I also think it's important to take a different look.

I am blessed to have a wonderful group of friends that represents a diverse cross-section of the population. I have watched their posts on social media, and sometimes their arguments with others to whom they are connected, and I am reminded how much they care. I am happy to have friends who treat me as an equal, who turn to me for advice, and to whom I know I can turn because they have stood beside me through thick and thin. They have traveled with me around the world and stood up for me at my wedding. The biggest compliment anyone has ever given my husband and me was at our wedding–our friend turned to us and said, "This wedding gives me hope for the world." This person saw people of all ages and races dancing together in celebration with pure happiness and no judgment. I believe one of the greatest lessons my parents taught my sister and me was to seek out friends from all backgrounds to broaden our knowledge, our awareness, and our perspective.

As one of two African American female CEOs running a non-minority-based national association in the construction industry, I recognize I wouldn't be here if it weren't for the support of white men. At the end of the day, they are the ones who hired me for all the jobs I've had in my career.

There is, of course, so much work that needs to be done, but I do think it is important to reflect on the good that is out there while also sharing ideas for improvement. As we move forward, here are three steps I recommend:

- **Recruiting for diversity must be intentional.**
  If you are a hiring manager or recruiter for a board, you have to make an effort to seek out diversity. If there is a large disparity within your current structure, you may need to look only at diverse candidates. Just because you don't know someone personally doesn't mean they won't be an asset to your team or your board. Please don't forget the Howard versus Heidi bias report and remember diversity is about more than just gender.[60]

- **Mentoring.**
  It is critical for leaders to serve as professional mentors. If you are a senior-level executive, make time to help pull someone forward. If you are trying to grow in your career and see someone you would like to learn from, you have to make the ask. But don't forget, you also have to share what you have

---

[60] Katsarou, Maria. "Women & the Leadership Labyrinth Howard vs Heidi." *Leadership Psychology Institute*. https://www.leadershippsychologyinstitute.com/women-the-leadership-labyrinth-howard-vs-heidi/. Accessed August 22, 2021.

to offer in return. Trust me, if you're a younger person, there are people who need to learn from your skills and talents just as much as you need to learn from them. Often, an executive with many years of experience still has content areas in which they need to grow.

- **Review who is in your social circle**.
  To people of all races, if you do not spend time outside of work with people who look and think differently than you, then you are not learning from them and they are not learning from you. We all must do more to build our personal networks with people of all cultural backgrounds. It starts when we are young, so if you have kids, make sure they spend time outside of school with children of different cultures. It's always said we fear what we don't understand. If we as a people don't break down our silos, we will never grow.

Don't Get Mad, Get Motivated!

Instead of getting mad when you face bias, get motivated to break down preconceived notions. If people view a group in a certain way, recognize *you* can be the one to impact the change. You have a unique opportunity to lead a paradigm shift in which you are seen as a leader and, in turn, it means others can be viewed as greater, too. All you have to do is be the best version of yourself and believe in yourself.

My husband and I were watching *American Idol* one night, and enjoyed listening to Alyssa Wray and Grace Kintsler, two powerhouse singers. As I'm in the middle of writing this book, the feedback given to Alyssa that night made me rewind and watch previous episodes. I wanted to note the differences in the ways they were coached, the messages that were shared, the areas of improvement suggested, and so on. The feedback felt personal, and it made me wonder... Why did they consistently tell the white woman who showcased her powerful vocals from start to finish that her performances were amazing while repeatedly advising the woman of color to reserve her vocal power until the end?

I believe one of the judges told Alyssa, "We know you have a gift. We know you have the power but save it...save it until the end." And they celebrated her for doing just that in her song selection and performance on her final night—a performance that, in the end, did not advance her forward. Now, that may just have been a fluke conversational note stating how they felt in the moment; but the fact that I remembered them giving her the same advice in at least two other episodes made me sad.

As I listened to those two amazing vocalists with very similar styles, I could not help but ask myself: *why tell one woman to hold back and the other to push forward?* The only difference in my eyes was black and white. It reminded me of the many times in my career when I was told to hold back. On more than one occasion, I was told, "Yes, yes, that's the right answer—but don't share it at this time. Hold back. Let somebody else shine. Let's give someone else an opportunity to come up with an idea before you share a winning idea again."

Why is it that women of color are often asked to hold back while white women are told to shine? And if you think I'm exaggerating, then go look at the data.[61] In our efforts to improve equity in corporate America, when companies have made changes to their male-to-female ratios, the females they placed in those positions were primarily, if not

---

[61] "Table 1: Employed and Experienced Unemployed Persons by Detailed Occupation, Sex, Race, and Hispanic or Latino Ethnicity, Annual Average 2019," *U.S. Bureau of Labor Statistics*, Current Population Survey (unpublished data) (2020).

entirely, white. Please note that one in five Americans are women of color.[62]

I bring up this topic purely to send a message to anyone who feels they don't have a voice or that they are being told it is not their time to shine:

Don't hold back...Shine bright and don't let other voices keep you from achieving the success you deserve.

Wake up on Monday morning, look at yourself in the mirror, and take the pledge that you will never get their coffee. When you believe you can break free from the status quo and prove your value is higher than you could ever imagine, you are deciding to take specific steps to view yourself as more than everybody else sees you. The next time you face a challenge or believe things aren't happening fast enough, think of Oprah and other leaders who continued to push forward regardless of what other people thought of them.

My career has been defined by people looking at who I am on the surface and deciding where I should be—not just professionally, but also socially. It isn't just the people today who do a double-take and say, "Oh, you're a CEO?" but also former classmates and even family members who, when I was younger, questioned the way I spoke and told me I was trying to be something I was not. Every day, I have decided to keep moving forward because I saw my value and would not allow others to plant the seed and cultivate a garden of self-doubt.

Even though unconscious bias is a reality, it is up to you to break the cycle and prove you are more than what you may appear to be on the surface. While deep-seated structural bias from some is common for so many, the good news is there is a new focus on working to challenge internal

---

[62] "Women of Color in the United States (Quick Take)." *Catalyst*, February 1, 2021. https://www.catalyst.org/research/women-of-color-in-the-united-states/. Accessed August 22, 2021.

bias. Many of the same people who were surprised I was an executive were the first to reach out to discuss strategy or business development. If I shut myself down and retreated because of the surface-level bias I encountered, I never would have stood tall and broken through that perception.

I recently watched an interview with Ann Mukherjee, Chair and CEO of Pernod Ricard North America. Ann is the first CEO who is a woman of color at a major alcohol brand. She shared her story and the challenges she faced in her life. She closed with a wonderful quote from her mother: "God put a gift in everyone. Your job is to figure out what that gift is and learn from it. Stop being perfect; it's in your imperfections that comes your strengths and your talent."[63]

Summary

- Recognize the intention behind a person's comment before responding.
- Recruiting for diversity must be intentional.
- Become a mentor.
- Diversify your social circle.
- Turn negative feedback into motivation for change.

---

[63] Villarreal, Mireya. CBS News. "Alcohol Devastated Her Childhood, Now Liquor Executive Takes on Irresponsible Drinking." *CBS News*. CBS Interactive, May 5, 2021. https://www.cbsnews.com/video/alcohol-devastated-her-childhood-now-liquor-executive-takes-on-irresponsible-drinking/. Accessed August 22, 2021.

Embrace a Growth Mindset

From the beginning of time, Black women were seen as the caretakers of their families and communities, always ready and able to take a step forward and address the issue at hand. This trait has become innate to us. Over twenty years ago, I was a young woman with a new career in the association sector. My boss often called upon me to step in and lend a hand when co-workers were unable to fulfill their duties. In some cases, I was thrust into projects, whether I had a say or not. My employer saw me as The Fixer, a catch-all person who would somehow get the work done without putting up a fight. To my advantage, every task thrown my way was an opportunity for me to challenge my potential.

My knowledge of program management and stakeholder relations began to evolve beyond my own expectations. I eventually began to master various core functions of association management. In reflection, my leadership development was in part due to my ability to challenge myself by learning and my willingness to assume new responsibilities. My employers' gains from my ability to deliver consistently was equally my gateway to recognitions, promotions, and job security.

As women, we can overcome the feeling of being taken advantage of in the workplace when we understand we are resilient beings, and always have been. Be open to unexpected opportunities in the workplace that will help you build on your experience and professional goals. Find ways to put your professional skills to the test so you are better informed of needed improvements. Keep progressing towards your leadership goals by challenging yourself to embrace a growth mindset.

—Sheri Sesay-Tuffour, PhD, CAE, CEO, Pediatric Nursing Certification Board

A Blueprint for Success

Throughout my career, I have been the first Black woman in each role I have held. My awareness of what this may mean for me came fairly early in my career. My second job out of college was managing a political action committee for an association in Virginia. Imagine being a 27-year-old Black woman having to convince your older, all-white political action committee (PAC) board of directors that changes were needed. I was scared. How do I do this? If I were too assertive, I would be called angry. If I were too passive, no one would listen to me. I decided that if I were armed with data and expertise, I could approach this situation in a measured and balanced way. So, I invited staff from the Federal Election Commission to present to the PAC board. I had one-on-one conversations with each board member. I presented data on how our PAC compared to similar groups. By the end of my time with this association, I managed to make some necessary changes and developed a good working relationship with my board. This experience gave me the blueprint to manage my career going forward.

Twenty years later, I am the executive director of a non-profit association. How did I get here? By making that measured stance work to my advantage. It made me a thought leader in my industry. It gave my opinions weight. As someone who has accomplished much in my career, it is now my responsibility to give back. I remind myself that I am standing on the shoulders of women who gave me a helping hand in the form of a reference, a job lead, or genuine advice on being the only woman of color in the room. For those of us who have reached the pinnacle of our careers, we need to be mindful that gatekeeping our expertise can hurt our younger counterparts. We did not reach this point in our careers on degrees and credentials alone. Mentoring is vital.

We have seen much progress in various industries, but the struggle and barriers remain. If you are a young woman of color, my advice to you is to surround yourself with mentors who are invested in your success. When you succeed, we all succeed. To my contemporaries, the next generation can benefit from the lessons we have learned. We have created our own tables. Let us help them create theirs.

—Stefanie Reeves, FASAE, CAE; Executive Director, Maryland Psychological Association

12

PRACTICE WELLNESS

In life, there will be stress and there will be challenges, but life is about how we face those conflicts and how we move forward. That is why it is essential we find time to practice mindfulness and focus on our wellness. Mindfulness means taking the time to unplug from the everyday notifications and updates and disconnect from the to-do list that is ever-running through your head.

Ever since I was young, I've found big bodies of water always bring me peace. I love to watch the flowing river or a waterfall and hear the sounds of waves crashing against the shore. Bodies of water cover nearly three quarters of this planet. When I look at the water, it reminds me just how small I am in the big scheme of things. Likewise, when I am suffering through conflict, water reminds me of how small my problems are.

Don't dwell on negative issues in the work environment. Find specific tools to address specific situations. Remember that most successful people gained their success by overcoming obstacles and setbacks. As time goes on, those experiences that were perceived as negative end up motivating us to push forward new ideas and break from our routine in order to lead us to a path of growth. I recommend you add something to your daily routine to start or end your day that provides a sense of peace and calm.

Here are five tips to wellness:

- **Develop healthy eating habits.**
  It seems like a simple statement, but healthy eating depends on how well you know how to plan for what you eat. I believe everything in life is about balance. So, when it comes to healthy eating, I think of it like my job. My goal is to try to eat healthy Monday through Friday and then enjoy myself on the weekend.

- **Make time for exercise**.
  Some people have developed a comprehensive workout regimen. They run every day or work out at the gym or on their indoor exercise bike at home. I am not that person. However, I discovered that if you exercise— even if it's just for 15 minutes a day—your health will improve. Because we have been working from home for an extended period of time due to the COVID-19 pandemic, I have encouraged my team to schedule walking meetings. Instead of sitting in the house on a call with a co-worker, as long as you don't have to show each other something on the computer screen, go for a walk. You will still accomplish the work conversation, and you will get some fresh air and feel better overall.

- **Drink more water**.
  Ever since I was a child, I was always told to drink more water. Staying hydrated is a key to your health and wellness. I was told to drink eight ounces of water eight times a day, although I've heard the amount of water you should drink actually depends on your weight. But for the past few years, I have focused on drinking at least 64 ounces a day. Studies show that staying hydrated helps your energy levels and performance and helps you

lose weight. In one study, dieters who drank 16.9 ounces of water before meals lost 44 percent more weight over 12 weeks as compared to dieters who didn't drink water before meals.[64]

- **Self-care is important**
  Give yourself time to relax your mind each day and, if possible, have dedicated time for yourself each week. Schedule time for yourself during your workday—for example, take a thirty-minute walk at lunch time. If I have meetings scheduled on my calendar during the workday, I don't miss them. The calendar reminds me what to do and I do it. It is important to schedule those needed breaks to ensure you take them. It could be as simple as scheduling time to read a book. Relaxing your mind helps you refocus when you return to work, so it benefits your company when you find balance in your day.

- **Spirituality**.
  Faith in a higher power can help bring balance and perspective in life. It is said that 84 percent of the world has faith in a higher power.[65] So this tip for wellness should come as no surprise. Spirituality or faith in something greater than yourself is extremely important as we find balance, perspective, and hope for the future.

---

[64] Dennis E.A., Ana Laura Dengo, Dana L. Comber, Kyle D. Flack, Jyoti Savla, Kevin P. Davy, and Brenda M. Davy. "Water Consumption Increases Weight Loss during a Hypocaloric Diet Intervention in Middle-Aged and Older Adults." *Obesity*, September 6, 2012. https://doi.org/10.1038/oby.2009.235. Accessed August 22, 2021.

[65] Harper, Jennifer. "84 percent of the world population has faith; a third are Christian." *The Washington Times*, December 23, 2012. https://www.washingtontimes.com/blog/watercooler/2012/dec/23/84-percent-world-population-has-faith-third-are-ch/. Accessed August 22, 2021.

Cast all your anxiety on him because he cares for you.
(1 Peter 5:7 NIV)
Trust in the Lord with all your heart; do not depend on your
own understanding. (Proverbs 3:5 NLT)

Spirituality for me has become a part of my everyday routine. Ever since I started making time each morning to find a quiet space and read my Bible, I have become a more positive, thoughtful, and happy person. Notice I said I had made time. It is really easy not to start your day in that quiet place and not take time to pray and offer your thanks for all the things you have been blessed with in your life. I have noticed that on days when I miss my quiet time and on days when I tell myself I'll get to it eventually, those are the days when I am not myself. Those are the days when I may struggle or stumble. I believe prayer or meditation is the best way to start any day.

There was a point in my life when I constantly used to say out loud to friends how thankful I was to have air in my lungs, working limbs on my body, and the ability to have a job and a place to live. They used to laugh when I made this comment, saying to me that I was a little too much. However, I think it is so important for each and every one of us to be grateful for what we have in our lives, and especially for the things we probably take for granted. How often do you sit back and say, "I am so lucky to have a job" instead of "This person at my office is annoying me"? How often do you say, "I'm too tired to go for a walk today" instead of "I'm so blessed to have both of my legs and the ability to walk if I so choose."

A few years ago, I went to watch a friend run in the Marine Corps Marathon. She said at mile 23 it gets really tough and that she would appreciate anyone who could come out and cheer her on. As I had never even contemplated the concept of running 26.2 miles, I obviously knew I was required to do my part and show up simply to cheer. That morning, I remember thinking I didn't want to go out that early. However, I did as I had promised and went to mile 23 to cheer her on.

What I found was inspiration. I saw people running from all ages, races, genders, and levels of ability. I saw people running with great speed and pride and style with one prosthetic leg, and I recognized and remembered all the blessings I had in my life. Here, I had been thinking I was too tired to stand on the sidelines and cheer when a person running past me with a prosthetic leg was smiling from ear to ear, feeling so blessed. That person recognized how important it was for him to be there and complete that marathon. There wasn't just one person with a handicap competing—there were many. When something is taken away, it is important to recognize and cherish the abilities you still have and move forward to conquer major goals.

Being thankful for what you still have after something of value has been taken away makes me think of the beginning of the COVID-19 pandemic. As I talked with friends or coworkers, I found one common thread: so many people missed the simple interactions at work they used to take for granted. People who traveled a lot for work suddenly missed the long lines, delayed flights, and airport food.

I say this to remind you to cherish what is in your life at this moment. You never know what will be taken away and you should appreciate all of your blessings.

Managing Mistakes

It is common for people to want to strive to achieve perfection. We want our work product to be without flaws and we want the same for the people who work for and with us. We should always aim for the stars when we are focused on developing new ideas, products, and services. Conduct all of your research, reach out to your network to help you build on new models or programs, and follow up with your team to complete a project.

We put our hearts and souls into our jobs and, from time to time, we will miss something. Maybe it is a typo on marketing materials you reviewed a hundred times or a release that went out without being properly vetted, or maybe you missed a meeting.

I do not like errors, from missed deadlines to any of the mistakes listed above, it eats at me when something goes wrong. The people on my team know this well: if I ask you to set a deadline, you had better not miss it—especially when it was your own deadline. Aim high but set a deadline that is realistic and accounts for errors or situations that are out of your control. Even when you plan appropriately, sometimes deadlines are missed or the situations out of your control are worse than you could have expected.

At the end of the day, we are all human. Although we endeavor never to miss a thing and always to produce perfect content, sometimes we will make mistakes. The important element is to find a way to recognize what went wrong, learn from that mistake, and move forward. When we reach those moments when we can't change the situation, we need to develop a way to move past it so we can focus on what comes next and not dwell on the error. Some people find it important to develop a routine for processing failure.

Here are a few tips:

- **Acknowledge the mistake**.
  Give yourself time to recognize what happened and allow yourself time to feel badly. Sometimes we just need to think about what went wrong and how it went wrong, so it doesn't happen again. Allow yourself the time to process.
- **Try to find a resolution**.
  Depending on the situation, some errors can be corrected. If you sent out an inaccurate press

release, send an updated version. Or if you miscalculated figures, recalculate and follow up.

- **Discuss the issue with your boss.**
  Be honest and take responsibility for your mistake. Companies know we are humans and not machines. Errors will happen. So be sure to let your boss know about the mistake as soon as possible and own it; don't try to blame others. If you are the lead on a project and it is behind schedule, take ownership of that delay and explain how you plan to adjust moving forward.

- **Find Your Cheerleader.**
  If you are lucky, you have a good friend or family member you can turn to when you hit the wall or make a mistake. It is always nice to be able to reach out to a friendly voice who will let you know that it's going to be ok. Whenever I make a mistake, because we all do, it is so important for me to call my cheerleaders. They are my voice of reason. They remind me of my success stories, tell me I am amazing and that this is just one hiccup and not to beat myself up about it. We all need that person to lean on, to remind us we are a rockstar, and to help us find the learning opportunity in this situation. If you don't have that cheerleader in your circle, come back to this section of the book when you need one and read these words:
  You are a rockstar! Everyone makes mistakes because we are all human. Sweep your error under the rug and move forward. I believe in you!

- **Move forward.**
  I have said it throughout this book: we must always focus on the future. When you make an error, acknowledge it, try to fix it, make sure you discuss it with your boss, and then move forward. We may want to dwell on the past, but we can't change what happened. All we can do is focus on what comes next and learn from these experiences to grow in our next.

Focus on What You Can Control

Early in my career, I contacted a friend to tell her about a bad day at work. When I think back, it was something silly about a missed deadline in a small brochure that didn't get printed in time. She listened to my assessment of what happened, sympathized, and told me everything would be okay. I thanked her and proceeded to ask about her day. My friend, who was a nurse, glanced down and said, "I didn't have a very good day, either." She stared blankly and whispered, "We lost a young boy." That moment was burned into my memory as a reminder that sometimes no matter what you are going through, someone else may be dealing with far greater challenges. It is a reminder to reassess and put some perspective on what you are dealing with compared to the overall big picture.

A lot of our frustration comes from the challenges in navigating the personalities, work, and general complexities of the modern workspace. Remember to take a deep breath and focus on what you can control. Here are five tips I wish I had known early in my career.

- **Don't take it personally.**
  You're not always going to agree with everyone you work with, but healthy debate is important in order to make decisions that are best for a company. Don't surround yourself only with people who agree with all your ideas, or you'll never allow yourself the opportunity to learn and grow.
- **Balance.**
  All work and no play. At my first association, I was often at the office until 9:00 p.m. on a Friday. That's what happens when you're in your early twenties and trying to prove yourself. As I look back, I'm not sure those consistent extended hours led me to where I am now. While I know my diligence was

a part of my early growth, I truly believe work-life balance leads to a more productive team.

- **Network, network, network!**

  I know for a fact I have grown in my roles because I stayed connected to my boss from my first association. Relationships are the key to professional growth. The best networking opportunity is getting involved in industry events. The people I met over the years at the American Society of Association Executives (ASAE) annual meeting have built my knowledge and network and allowed me to give back. When I say *network*, I don't just mean making friends with like-minded individuals. I mean building relationships with people in similar and higher-level roles who can provide a broader perspective on efficiencies in what you do and how to innovate.

- **Back up your opinion with data.**

  I can't count the number of times that I've heard someone say, "What we oughta do is..." But when you ask them why or how the company will grow or financially benefit, they don't have an answer. Your opinion is just your opinion until you've backed it up with data. It's not just about having good ideas, it's about backing them up with the research and financials to validate that argument. Don't be afraid to prove yourself. Even if it doesn't go your way, people will respect you've done the legwork.

- **No one ever gets promoted for knowing all the gossip.**

  Younger employees: If you're new, fresh out of college, and excited about your career, don't get mixed up in office politics. Just do your best and show your work. While it's tempting to listen and take part in all the stories, trust me, management is listening. No one wants to promote the office gossip.

Summary

- Don't dwell on negative issues.
- Take care of your body with healthy eating, hydration, and exercise.
- Find a spirituality routine.
- Don't take your health for granted.
- Manage mistakes through acknowledgement and resolution and by moving forward.
- Focus on what you can control.

Self-Care Is Not Selfish

I used to think that things like breaks during your workday, exercise, and eight hours of sleep each night were nice-to-haves if you were somehow able to squeeze it all in around the demands of full-time careers, kids, partners, and adulting, in general. But then I had a nervous breakdown followed by an ER visit and short-term medical leave in 2018 after running myself into the ground leading a huge team on an unwieldy, ambiguously defined work project. The toxic combination of a month of one or two hours of sleep nightly, 18- to 20-hour workdays, and little else to nourish me aside from coffee and Cheez-Its drove me to a breaking point. In the aftermath—and with the help of a great therapist—I had a revelation: all those things I had thought were just nice to have were actually critical to sustaining my energy and impact across every aspect of my life. If I'm not continuously, vigilantly prioritizing self-care and saying no when necessary, I cannot bring my best. Today, I manage my energy—physically, emotionally, and mentally—by leveraging scientifically based guidance from

The Energy Project.[66] I co-create resilience plans with my teams focused on five key behaviors:

- Do your most important work when you first get to the office for an uninterrupted stretch of sixty to ninety minutes and then take a renewal break.
- Get up from your desk at lunchtime for at least thirty minutes and do some type of movement.
- After ninety minutes of work, take a break for at least five minutes. If that isn't possible, do one minute of deep breathing to clear your bloodstream of stress hormones.
- When you stop working for the day, do something that allows you to transition mentally and emotionally between work and home.
- Set a pre-sleep routine and a bedtime that ensures you get at least seven hours of sleep.

Well-being is a leadership skill that enables retention and positively contributes to your bottom line. You must learn it, practice it and spread it!

—Alicia Downey Bowman, PMP, HR Management Consultant

---

[66] More information can be found at https://theenergyproject.com/.

Epilogue–Life Lessons from My Three-Year-Old

This has been a fascinating time of discovery as I've watched my daughter grow over the past three years. Watching the process by which she had to learn to turn over, crawl, walk and then run has me re-evaluating the definition of determination. No matter how challenging things seem to be, human beings are instilled with the belief they will eventually succeed. I've watched my daughter bump her head and fall down, but no matter how long it takes, she always gets back up again and keeps trying.

How is it that we all start off so determined and then somehow, later in life, we give up so easily? Watching my daughter interact with the world around her has reminded me of the things we all need to remember at work, day in and day out.

Those lessons are

- Have determination
- Try new things
- Find happiness

How often do we have that great idea to save costs or increase efficiency and give up after one informal conversation with our boss? We hang our heads in shame and think, "Well, the boss said no... Ahh, they'll never listen."

Instead of shrugging your shoulders, complaining, and searching for a company where they'll listen to your ideas, why don't you rethink your presentation?

- Did you give the written reasons why your idea will save money?
- Did you research the relevant data that backs up your proposed change?

How many of us take a long lunch or a thirty-minute coffee break to complain about company culture and how the higher ups don't listen to important ideas when a ten-minute Google search to find some data would change the entire framework of the idea we are presenting?

When we are born into this world, we do not understand others cannot be responsible for our happiness. My daughter must walk with her own legs and her own feet, and if she does not, there is no one else to blame. She has a constant desire to say her ABCs, practice counting, and learn new phrases. She believes she can do anything by herself and needs no assistance. Proper growth, not just as a human being, but in work and life, requires balance. Looking at your potential is essential to revealing the possibility of what's to come in your life. If you look at things from a negative light, or always look at the glass as half empty, how will you grow and succeed? My daughter's favorite song is Shakira's "Try Everything." I listen to the words with a new focus these days.

The purpose of this book is to open up dialogue to those who are hesitant to share their great ideas and also to consider the obstacles that are organizational, social, and societal. It's for the fathers who don't want to repeat ideas or phrases that make their daughters feel as if they are less capable and for the executives who are already leaders and want to strive to that next step. It's for the aunts, uncles, and neighbors who are training the next generation. It's for us to recognize that the preconceptions that are built within men and women are established at a very young age. It's for the future business owners who will be impacted by conscious and unconscious bias from the moment they seek funding to the moment they present their business plans. We must share the message that *everyone* is strong, smart, and capable—*not just boys*—and that we must not to doubt anyone because of their sex. This book isn't just for women getting started, it's for people in the middle of their careers and those in the twilight of their careers who are bringing along the next generation. Writing a book on leadership is not simply about teaching skills; it's also about all the soft, subtle ways we are discouraged from reaching our full potential. I wrote in a previous chapter this statement, which is truly for all women reading this book:

Don't hold back...Shine bright and don't let other voices keep you from achieving the success you deserve. Never get their coffee and be empowered to showcase fearless leadership!

Acknowledgements

I must start by acknowledging that this book would have never seen the light of day if not for my sweet and thoughtful husband, Tim. Many years ago, when we were commuting together, if I was driving and sharing my thoughts about the workday or describing things I have seen or experienced, he would take notes. About a year later, he shared what he had written from my daily chatter and said, "Other women need to hear what you are saying. You should turn this into a book." Later, when a professional mentor, Conrad Woody, advised me to share my thought leadership, I began to share some of this content on LinkedIn. After gathering feedback from the community, I learned I should continue to share knowledge with others and developed what later became the manuscript for this book. But again, my husband Tim continued to encourage me, making sure I made time to write or offering to take notes while I talked (my favorite way to write).

Thanks to the team at Leaders Press for recognizing my content online and recommending that I publish a book. To my project managers, Matt Dunn and Jessa Bulawin thanks for keeping me on track and working with me and your design team through various iterations of book covers. Thanks to my editor, Anna Paige, and her exceptional eye for detail, organization of thoughts, and pulling out a deeper message from my experiences I may have struggled to describe.

The book did not truly take shape until my amazing network of exceptional female leaders offered to share their stories. Once I connected their message to the chapters, that is when I truly became excited about what the book could be.

I also want to take this moment to express my thanks to those who hired me for my skill, talent, and potential, and not my race. To Mark Pursell, who hired me at my first association and brought me along to multiple companies, thanks for always being in my corner. To my former board members who have wholeheartedly encouraged me and appreciated my ideas, I offer you my thanks. I know not everyone has supported me in previous roles and sometimes I had to fight to do what was best for the company, but even those moments made me a stronger person. I am also grateful to my friend Betty Whitaker and professional colleagues who over the years trained and mentored me and backed my ideas when others wouldn't. Their support is what kept me going and driving for success.

I would be remiss to not thank my previous and current board members, who trusted that I was the right person for the company. To be selected as an African American female CEO, in the built environment, gives me hope that we as a community can grow in diversity, equity, and inclusion. Last but not least, I must, of course, thank my mother, who is my spiritual counselor, for all of her unconditional love and prayers.

About the Author

L akisha Ann Woods is a CEO, board member, Chair of the American Society of Association Executives Foundation (ASAE), and a global thought leader who frequently speaks about the importance of female leadership and equity. Having spent much of her career in leadership positions representing the construction industry, she considers diversifying the workforce and elevating and celebrating female and diverse leaders to be a critical mission and passion project. A self-proclaimed military brat, her father's service in the U.S. Air Force brought the family around the world and taught her to adapt quickly. She is a keynote speaker and has participated on panels at numerous national and international industry events. Lakisha holds a Bachelor of Science from the University of Maryland in College Park and lives with her supportive husband and daughter in Howard County, Maryland.

https://lakishawoods.com/bonus

https://lakishawoods.com/bonus